1295

BV
4811
.F584
2003

S0-ATF-127

OTHER BOOKS BY MARCIA FORD

Memoir of a Misfit

Restless Pilgrim: The Spiritual Journey of Bob Dylan

Checklist for Life for Teens

God's Little Pocket Devotional

God's Little Pocket Devotional for Teens

Shout to the Lord

Charisma Reports: The Brownsville Revival

Meditations for Misfits

FINDING YOUR PLACE IN THE FAMILY OF GOD

Marcia Ford

JOSSEY-BASS
A Wiley Imprint
www.josseybass.com

Published by Jossey-Bass
A Wiley Imprint
989 Market Street, San Francisco, CA 94103   www.josseybass.com

Jossey-Bass books and products are available through most bookstores. To contact Jossey-Bass directly call our Customer Care Department within the United States at (800) 956-7739, outside the United States at (317) 572-3993 or fax (317) 572-4002.

Jossey-Bass also publishes its books in a variety of electronic formats. Some content that appears in print may not be available in electronic books.

Credits are on page 164.

Book design by Suzanne Albertson

Library of Congress Cataloging-in-Publication Data
Ford, Marcia.
  Meditations for misfits : finding your place in the family of God / Marcia Ford.— 1st ed.
    p.   cm.
  Includes bibliographical references.
  ISBN 0-7879-6400-X (alk. paper)
  1. Meditations. I. Title.
BV4811 .F586 2003
242—dc21   2002013073

Printed in the United States of America
FIRST EDITION
HB Printing   10 9 8 7 6 5 4 3 2 1

Contents

To Elizabeth and Sarah

Introduction

I f you're a spiritual misfit like me, you've likely experienced a somewhat complicated relationship with God and with the church. It takes a fair amount of courage and tenacity to hold on to your faith when you feel as if everyone is looking at you funny—including God. What makes it worse is when you come to the conclusion that you are utterly alone. No one else seems to think or act or believe the way you do. Everyone else appears to fit in.

Three things you need to know: You are mistaken in the belief that you are alone. You are correct in the belief that no one else thinks or acts or believes the way you do. And whether or not anyone else actually does fit in is irrelevant.

After a lifetime of alternately fighting and hiding and strutting out my misfit nature, I have come to not only accept my misfittedness but also embrace it. In befriending my eccentricity, I discovered an authentic life—a life free from the pretense of trying to be someone I am not, from the overwhelming sense of isolation from God and the dominant culture, and from concern about the disapproval—whether perceived or genuine—of other people.

Through these meditations, and a companion book, *Memoir of a Misfit*, I hope that you will come to see that you are not alone. You'll soon realize that the world is populated with many quirky individuals who manage to live productive lives despite their inability to conform to the behavioral demands of the society in which they live. Some of them are the creative souls whose words I quote in the meditations, but many more are the cooks and shopkeepers and teachers and farmers and cowboys who creatively—and often painfully—step to the "measured and far away" beat of that different drummer that Henry David Thoreau gave life to. Their names may not appear on these pages, but their impact on my life has been significant. By their example, I've learned to live as a productive misfit in a society that can be relentlessly unforgiving of offbeat personalities.

Apart from the obsessive-compulsives in our midst who can't live without a normal routine, most misfits cannot abide anything resembling one. In light of that, I realized early on that it was pointless to try to squeeze these meditations into a traditional thirty-day or fifty-two-week or an exceedingly laughable 365-day format. I also had far too many favorite quotes by C. S. Lewis, and if I was going to stick to a "normal" format, I didn't want to quote the same author twice. So I decided to forget normal and go with fifty-three meditations, to free you from any threat of a scheduling restriction and to satisfy my need to give Lewis an extra hearing.

May God give you the courage and tenacity to hold on not only to your faith but also to every idiosyncrasy that makes you the person you are, the person He intended you to be.

—*Marcia Ford*

Meditations for Misfits

SPACES IN YOUR SOUL

The wind pounding on the north side of the house,
pounding down off the Dakotas a thousand miles away and
across the plains which were icy and pearl-blind with the snow
polished hard under the wind and glimmering in the dark. . . .

ROBERT PENN WARREN

Many people can tell you where they were and who they were with and what the weather was like the first time they heard a groundbreaking album like *Sgt. Pepper's Lonely Hearts Club Band*. Not me. I remember every detail of the moment I first read certain words, like the ones quoted above. At the time, I was sitting cross-legged on a narrow, lumpy bed, halfheartedly reading Robert Penn Warren's *All the King's Men* for an American lit class in college, when this one sentence—condensed to a considerable degree—stopped me cold, so to speak. The imagery tugged at some ancient, haunting memory, something so distant and yet so familiar. Twenty-five years later, the words still resonate with me.

When you experience moments like that, the predictability of your life vanishes, and you're caught off guard by something so mysterious that time shuts down. Once time resumes, you want to share this profound and precious discovery, so you naively open up your thoughts to a supposed soul mate. And you are unprepared for the response you get. "That's nice," your friend says, groping for a tactful way to rein you back in. "Yeah, that sounds like a cold place," another may say, missing the point. But mostly, you get the impression your friend is wondering, *Is she nuts or what?*

That's why I've never expressed my feelings about that sentence until now. By the time I encountered Robert Penn Warren, I had come to expect bewilderment whenever I exposed my deepest thoughts to others. And it's probably just as well that I can't see your reaction now. Maybe as you read along you started rolling your eyes or laughing out loud—or maybe you whispered, "Yes, yes," because you too caught the magic in Penn Warren's words.

Whether it was a string of words on a page or an image from a movie or a pen-and-ink sketch you spied at a flea market, you've experienced something— no doubt, more than one thing—that has pierced your soul and lodged there, echoing its message to you at the unlikeliest of times. It filled up a space inside that you weren't aware of until that unbidden image came to stay. Those spaces in your soul are no mistake of creation; God seems to have intentionally left those spaces there, knowing that one day an impression would leave you so awestruck that you would need a vacant chamber in which to store it.

It doesn't matter whether anyone else on the planet "gets" what you get. It's yours to treasure, to keep hidden in a place where only you and God can gain access. In time, you'll cherish those experiences that set you apart from others, as you draw near to your one true soul mate—the Spirit of God.

For who among men knows the thoughts of a man except the man's spirit within him? In the same way no one knows the thoughts of God except the Spirit of God.

1 Corinthians 2:11

Lord, thank You for the hidden places that only You and I share. Grant me the grace to open up my soul and share my deepest thoughts with You.

VIEW FROM THE VALLEY

One sees great things from the valley;
only small things from the peak.

G. K. CHESTERTON

One of the greatest rewards you get when you befriend your misfit nature is the freedom to live an unconventional life—and think in an unconventional way. The unconventional G. K. Chesterton, an astonishing thinker, writer, and eccentric, tended to turn the rocks of conventional wisdom over and reveal the truth that lay underneath. Never was he better at that than when he revealed the truth of Scripture.

Chesterton got it right. As the masses rush to seek mountaintop experiences—anything to escape the despair of the lowlands—God is revealing great truths to those who are mired in the valley. They—we—may not appreciate it at the time. Our valley life seems endless; we begin to get choosy about the Scriptures we believe are true, starting with 2 Peter 3:8, which reminds us that to God, one day is like a thousand years. We convince ourselves that we're doomed, condemned to a life sentence as bottom dwellers in full view of those spiritual beings looking for all the world like an expedition making a final assault on Everest.

We forget that it was God who carved out the valleys, that they are every bit as much a part of His domain as the mountains are. In that endearing way He has of reminding us who's boss, God offers up a verse that shows what happens to those who fail to recognize His presence everywhere. It's a straightforward, ho-hum kind of verse you might not think twice about, but look at the truth beneath that rock: "This is what the LORD says: 'Because the Arameans think the LORD is a god of the hills and not a god of the valleys, I will deliver this vast army into your hands, and you will know that I am the LORD'" (1 Kings 20:28). The Arameans did not see God at work in both the hills and the valleys, and so the Israelites—God's army—defeated them.

As you languish in the valley, wondering if you'll ever savor the view from the mountaintop, the God of the valley is very much at work in your life. He's preparing you for the ascent, and often the training will be downright painful. Once again, you'll need to flip conventional wisdom over and resist the temptation to attribute your pain to Satan and his minions. The truth is that sometimes divine discipline can hurt like nothing else can—but oh, the reward, the "harvest of righteousness and peace" (Hebrews 12:11).

No one stays on the mountaintop for very long. Moses lasted forty days, but God made him return to the valley to implement the lessons he learned on Mount Sinai. And Everest climbers hardly enjoy the view from the top; they quickly pose for a photo to prove they reached the summit and then hightail it off the peak before their oxygen—or their luck—runs out. In short, mountaintop experiences aren't always what they're cracked up to be. Chesterton would no doubt agree.

❧

> I lift up my eyes to the hills—
> where does my help come from?
> My help comes from the LORD,
> the Maker of heaven and earth.
> *Psalm 121:1–2*

Lord, keep me from resisting Your work in my life when I feel stuck in the valley. Help me to see the great things You are trying to show me.

DEEP RESERVOIR

*When the ever creative soul is allowed to rise up
from the deep reservoir of life that is its home, we become
unpredictable and not easily squeezed into narrow
expectations of what a person should be. In the flush
of the soul's vitality, we become eccentric.*

THOMAS MOORE

Eccentric. That's what we misfits are, really. But it's not that we're difficult or insane. We're eccentric because we've done just what Thomas Moore describes: We've allowed our soul to rise up from the reservoir within us, and the life we live draws its creative energy from the depth of our being. It's our creativity that gets us in trouble, of course: We think and act and behave creatively, uniquely, disregarding all those signals along the way warning us that we're about to veer off the prescribed course of mainstream culture.

So be it. If you've become unpredictable, even to yourself, that's cause for celebration, not concern. The flush of your soul's vitality demonstrates not only that you're alive but also that you're fully alive, open to every possibility and side-track and rabbit trail spread out over the landscape before you. Let others hold to the narrow expectations of what a person should be; theirs is a life journey on an interstate highway, highly efficient but dreadfully predictable and routine. Your life journey will take you onto the side streets that lead to the heart of a city with all its crying need, its wealth, its poverty, its hurting people—or onto the back roads that lead to a wilderness where you will discover hiking trails and winding paths that guide you toward deep canyons and thick forests where you can get blissfully lost in yourself and in the Spirit of God.

Likewise, your daily interior journey takes you places where others fear to tread. Your thoughts meander in and out of reality, making so many twists and turns that you often cannot trace the complex course of an idea that seemed so simple in its conception. If you happen to be talking when the course goes haywire—which it will at times—you find yourself in big conversational trouble, because you have no clue how the sentence you started is going to end up. If that occurs often enough, the resulting frustration and embarrassment can threaten to drive you to withdraw from ordinary interaction with ordinary people. But those ordinary people need you, a remarkable, extraordinary person, to keep them on their toes and show them what it means to be fully alive. Unless you're called to be a recluse, you're called to share your life in the Spirit with others. You can't do that in isolation.

You'll never fit the mold of the expectations of others. When your mind and your spirit refuse to behave in a way that's acceptable to others—in public, no less—remember Moore's point: You are eccentric and unpredictable in part because you have allowed your creativity to surface. Your ever creative soul was designed to break the mold—not fit into it.

We live in this world, but we don't act like its people.
2 Corinthians 10:3 (CEV)

Lord, I need to see myself as a remarkable, extraordinary person who has something of value to offer to the world around me. Help me resist the temptation to isolate myself from others.

IMMERSED IN HUMANITY

You are not a human being in search of spiritual experience.
You are a spiritual being immersed in a human experience.

PIERRE TEILHARD DE CHARDIN

Think for a moment about the way you view your existence. Your thoughts may go something like this: You have a body that keeps all the tangible parts of you in one place, more or less. And you have a brain that houses your thoughts and controls your impulses, also more or less. Finally, you have this thing that you can't see or touch but is the real you, and some people call it your spirit, and others call it your soul, a distinction that has touched off an everlasting debate among theologians and philosophers. Meanwhile, you take all this for granted. All you know is, you are a person who longs for spiritual experience.

Then along comes Pierre Teilhard de Chardin, whose name you hope you'll never have to try to pronounce in public, and he knocks you upside the head by telling you you've got it all wrong. You are a spiritual being, he says, and you exist in the midst of an eternal spiritual experience; there's no need for you to go searching for it. Your only problem is that once you took on a physical body and became immersed in human experience, you gave more attention to your humanity than to your spirituality.

You can make that as simple or as complicated as you care to; Teilhard's words are basically a succinct expression of the biblical definition of life. Life is spirit, Jesus said in the Gospel of John, adding the radical thought that the body is useless. What He's saying is that your body is useless when it comes to your eternal existence. It serves an earthly purpose, but it's not you. The real you is spirit, and your real experience is spiritual. Your body is the clothing you wear for the short time you're immersed in this human experience

Great, you think. *And this is supposed to change my life. . . . How?* To begin with, you can call off the spiritual search, provided you already have a relationship with God. He is Spirit and you are spirit, and whatever you do to get to know Him better, and to get to know your real self better, contributes to the priceless Spirit-spirit relationship you already have. That doesn't mean you should hunker down in a cave and spend every waking moment in prayer and meditation, though please feel free. It also doesn't mean you must avoid conferences and seminars and workshops on spirituality (though, once again, please feel free). It does mean you don't need to do any of that to have a genuine spiritual experience. You're already having one.

As you get to know yourself, your true nature will unfold, and you will discover the unique way God communicates with you. Your discovery may be as profound as Moses' encounter with God on Mount Sinai, as practical as switching to a new translation of the Bible, or as sacred as altering the very way you worship God.

∾

"Life is spiritual. Your physical existence doesn't contribute to that life. The words that I have spoken to you are spiritual. They are life."

John 6:63 (GOD'S WORD)

Lord, never let me forget that my life is lived in the spirit and not in the flesh, that my human nature is subject to my spirit and not the other way around. Give me the grace to appreciate my spiritual nature.

THE SLIGHTEST SOUND

I throw myself down in my chamber, and I call in, and
invite God, and his Angels thither, and when they are there,
I neglect God and his Angels, for the noise of a fly, for the
rattling of a coach, for the whining of a door.

JOHN DONNE

If you're the type who finds it difficult to concentrate when you attempt to come into the presence of God, you should be able to take some comfort in these words penned by John Donne. He was one of the greatest spiritual poets that ever lived, and yet he confessed to being distracted by the slightest sound. We may think we have it much worse than he did, what with the unceasing sounds made by technological wonders that hum and buzz and whir and ring and make an announcement whenever "You've got mail!" But we can't use that as an excuse, because ever since God created the second human being way back in the Garden, we've faced distraction. There really is nothing new under the sun.

Because you're already accustomed to doing things slightly differently from the way everybody else does them, you might want to try doing exactly the opposite of what you think you should do when little things turn your attention from "God and his Angels." You probably think you should try to concentrate harder, until you're squinting your already shut eyes even tighter, and clenching your jaws and your fists so hard that if nothing else, you'd frighten the dickens out of anything that dared to try to distract you. But by then, you've lost whatever peace you might have had, and you're not exactly in the right frame of mind to pray or meditate or bask in the presence of God anymore.

The opposite approach would be to relax, to expect God to help you enter into His presence with your mind and spirit fully engaged. Then, when a host of little noises begin to unite in an unmistakable effort to attract your attention, give it to them—your attention, that is. But briefly, very briefly. When a mosquito starts to buzz nearby, thank God for His creation and remind Him that you'd really like to know why He made mosquitoes in the first place (swatting it will prove that you're serious about wanting an answer, that this is not a rhetorical question). If, like Donne, you're distracted by the "rattling of a coach," or the sound of a car driving by, pray for the safety and spiritual lives of those in the car. And if the irritation of a squeaky door unhinges you, well, make a quick mental note to oil it. Then, no matter what the nature of the distraction, bid it farewell and turn your attention back to your heart's desire—precious time alone with God.

Contrary to the image some people have of God, your loving Father is not a celestial scorekeeper who rates your performance each time you pray. He's not standing behind a lectern saying, "Well, your heart was right, but I have no choice but to give you a D in concentration. You'll have to try to do better next time." He wants you to be anxious for nothing—and that includes the inevitable distractions of life.

Do not be anxious for anything, but in everything, by prayer and petition, with thanksgiving, present your requests to God.
Philippians 4:6

Father, thank You for Your goodness and mercy toward me. Keep me mindful of the truth that You always delight in me, even when I turn my attention to momentary distractions.

WILD AND WONDERFUL

What would the world be, once bereft
Of wet and wildness? Let them be left,
O let them be left, wildness and wet;
Long live the weeds and the wilderness yet.

GERALD MANLEY HOPKINS

What would the world be without us, the wild ones who would like others to just let us be? It would certainly become a neat and tidy and efficient place. And it would be utterly boring. Those who would prefer a boring but tidy world see us as weeds, sprouting up where we're not wanted; you just know that they wouldn't mind mowing us down if they could. What they may not realize is that there's actually no difference between a weed and a wildflower. Some "weeds" are even beautiful and useful and necessary. So maybe we're not cultivated or hybridized, but we grow wild and wonderful like a desert in bloom.

Author Robert Fulghum once pointed out that if dandelions weren't so tough and ubiquitous, people would treasure them. But because dandelions "are everywhere and don't need us and kind of do what they please," people regard them as weeds and try to get rid of them. Sound familiar? Misfits are everywhere, and if we're true to ourselves, we don't need other people to validate our identity. And we pretty much do what we please, which is exactly what prevents us from fitting in to a well-ordered society that loves the uniformity of a perfectly manicured lawn.

It's mostly the poets, the creative souls, who seem to recognize the value of those plants that others call weeds. James Russell Lowell described a weed as a flower in disguise; Ralph Waldo Emerson, a plant of undiscovered virtue. Henry David Thoreau chastised those who cheapen the significance of weeds, which he believed were placed on earth to express a specific thought or mood. Apply those descriptions to yourself, and you'll begin to see your uniqueness as a lofty and noble calling and not a lowly and miserable curse.

We also have lots of botanists on our side. Several years ago, a group of three hundred scientists triumphantly ended a $70 million project with the discovery that one "weed" that had been deemed useless was in fact a model organism whose genetic code holds information vital to our understanding of the world's ecosystems. No wonder some botanists are annoyed when gardeners treat weeds like unwanted and uninvited guests. Think about that the next time you're treated like a useless, unwanted, uninvited guest. You are a model organism that holds vital clues to the understanding of humanity, and no one has to pay $70 million for that bit of information. You can tell them for free.

As always, our most important and powerful advocate is our Creator. He saw to it that the land produced "plants bearing seed according to their kinds. . . .

And God saw that it was good" (Genesis 1:12). If you believe God created every-thing, then you have to believe God created those plants that the uninitiated call weeds—and He considered them good. Good! Not unwanted. Not unin-vited. Not useless. But good.

> He has made everything beautiful in its time. He has also set eternity in
> the hearts of men; yet they cannot fathom what God has done from
> beginning to end.
>
> *Ecclesiastes 3:11*

Lord, You have made me to be a worthwhile, valuable person. I may not be able to fathom what You have done in my life from beginning to end, but I gratefully thank You all the same.

THE YEARNING WITHIN

Each creature God made
Must live in its own true nature;
How could I resist my nature,
that lives for oneness with God?

MECHTHILD OF MAGDEBURG

$\mathcal{M}$echthild, a thirteenth-century mystic, chose a radical course for her journey toward oneness with God: a monastic life devoted not only to prayer but also to extreme hardship and deprivation in an effort to destroy the sin that she believed separated her from God. Others have followed a similar course, taking Paul's mention of disciplining his body to an extreme. That's the way their true nature was inclined to experience oneness with God.

I don't know about you, but I'm thankful that my true nature operates in a different way. And yet my nature does desire oneness with God, though phrasing my desire in those terms can open a huge can of theological worms. Better to call it communion with God. Whatever it is, I've resisted it more than I've pursued it, sometimes denying the yearning through busyness or indifference or worldliness or spiritual laziness. But most often, I'd have to say that I denied the yearning through a crushing sense of defeat. I didn't measure up, no matter how disciplined or severe my religious practices were. Who was I to think I could achieve genuine communion with God? And what made me think He would want me to?

After I gave in to that defeat, though, my true nature was still there, still yearning, still unsatisfied. I became an expert at silencing the cries I heard from within. When I finally stopped the game of denial that I was playing with myself, I was able to see that my attempts at communion with God were blocked not by Him or by my unworthiness but by my own striving for some mystical experience. Experience, I've learned, is just experience. It can certainly involve the presence of God in a way that makes Him seem more real and accessible. But experience is not God, who is always real and always accessible. Unadorned contemplation of God Himself led me to God Himself, much to my surprise.

Whenever we resist our true nature, we border on living a lie, many times for the sake of others. People who live an authentic life, a life that aligns with their true nature, make other people very nervous. That creates a tension that tempts us to back off and settle for less than who we truly are. We need the courage and determination of all of the Mechthilds of religious history, those who followed their own unique way of expressing their true nature without regard for what others thought of them. Listen to the cry within you, the yearning you have for communion with God. Discover the way your true nature can best achieve the communion you long for. Ask God to help you fearlessly live an authentic life, the life He made you to live.

> I will praise you because I am fearfully and wonderfully made;
> your works are wonderful,
> my soul knows that very well.
>
> *Psalm 139:14*

Lord, teach me to pursue You and not a spiritual experience, no matter how right it seems. Give me the grace to be true to myself, believing that I have been wonderfully made by You.

WHO YOU REALLY ARE

———————

Nothing is a greater impediment to being on good terms
with others than being ill at ease with yourself.

HONORÉ DE BALZAC

ar be it from me to edit the great Balzac, but I will annotate his comment above. I would add that nothing—other than sin—is a greater impediment to being on good terms with God than being ill at ease with yourself. Our Christian tradition is so outwardly focused—and to a certain extent, rightly so—that we consider self-reflection to be narcissistic and selfish. We're exhorted to sacrificially give ourselves to God and to others. The problem is that all too often, we don't know what we're giving, because we don't really know ourselves.

Like many people, the last thing I wanted to do was look deep into my soul to discover who I really was. What I saw on the surface was bad enough! No, thanks; I would leave the soul-searching to others who stood a better chance of finding buried treasure deep within their own normal selves. Me, I figured I would find a mound of toxic, putrefied garbage.

Then God pulled a fast one on me. He lured me to a place where I would be alone for the better part of a week. At first, that didn't seem so bad. I thought I would welcome the solitude. But I had never experienced genuine solitude — no television, no radio, no distractions. Just God and me, alone in a small room with a bed, a chair, a desk, and a lamp.

Under the guidance of a spiritual leader, I gradually allowed God to begin to show me who I really am. Though the hours at times seemed endless, trust me, a week just gets you started on the journey toward self-discovery. But that was enough for Him to help me begin to see that maybe, just maybe, I'm not all that bad. Since then, I have become more comfortable with my eccentric self and less ill at ease with others. Better yet, I am on great terms with God, now that I have learned to be content with who I am.

You don't need to lock yourself in a monastic cell to become better acquainted with yourself. But you do need to turn down the noise in your mind and in your life so you can hear your private thoughts and allow God to show you who you are inside. Pop psychologists take this kind of practice to an extreme, promoting self-love and self-knowledge as the purpose of life and the cure for all its ills. It's neither. As you read Scripture, you realize that becoming content with who you are is a way of honoring God. Your newfound transparency allows you to approach Him — and the people around you — with a fearless and confident openness.

按

I am not saying this because I am in need, for I have learned to be content whatever the circumstances.

Philippians 4:11

Father, give me the grace to be unafraid to discover the person You made me to be. Teach me how to be content with myself, transparent with You, and comfortable in the presence of others.

CLOSE TO THE FLOOR

━━ ▬ ▬ ▬ ━━

I never knew God lived so close to the floor.

SHEILA WALSH

There's one place where I can always be sure that God is with me, whether I feel His presence or not. It's not the kind of place you would normally associate with the presence of God, like an altar rail in a cathedral or a quiet refuge in the woods. It's the floor, where I end up when there's nowhere left to go.

That's where I was on the morning I thought God and I had gone our separate ways. There, on a hotel room floor, I realized we were at an impasse. Tired of the struggle and too drained to cry, I silently called it quits.

It was the best thing that could have happened to me at that time.

I did not sense God's presence in that room. Truth is, I didn't sense His existence anywhere in the universe. I had committed what to some Christians would be a heresy: I gave in to the depression that I had not identified yet. Eventually, I would look depression square in the face, acknowledge it, thank God for it, and begin to embrace it. Only then would I be able to get the medical help I needed and allow God to expose the causes of my despair so the healing process could begin.

Feeling out of step with the rest of the world is enough to drive anyone to the floor in misery. But when carpet time characterizes a lifestyle rather than an occasional bout of the blues, it's time to admit to a larger problem. Christians find this especially difficult, because we're supposed to have not only the righteousness and peace that eludes us but also an inordinate amount of joy. So we deny our depression, allowing it to fester below the surface of our lives where it does its silent damage. If we as much as hint that we're depressed, well-meaning believers—who clearly never experienced clinical depression—tell us to snap out of it or pray against it or fight it like crazy. Not bad advice, but totally useless, because there's no snap or prayer or fight left in us. It's like telling a paralytic to get moving.

By giving in to depression, I did not resign myself to it. I simply quit fighting it, even though I had no idea whether any good would come of giving up the fight. Frankly, I didn't care. I had reached a "whatever" place. And although I did not say that word to God, He took my "whatever" attitude as a code word for the words I could not utter: *I've reached the end of me. I don't care what happens to me anymore.* Only He pulled rank and put a postscript in my mouth, granting Himself permission to heal me: *P.S. Oh, and God, go ahead and do whatever You want to with me.* He had been right there with me on the floor, listening to my heart all along.

If your inability to fit in has caused you to despair, you may think your depression has separated you from God. It has not. And that's biblical. Like the apostle Paul, I am convinced that "neither death, nor life ... nor depth"—nor depression—"nor anything else in all creation, will be able to separate us from the love of God that is in Christ Jesus our Lord" (Romans 8:38–39).

> Why are you downcast, O my soul?
> Why so disturbed within me?
> Put your hope in God,
> for I will yet praise him,
> my Savior and my God.
> *Psalm 42:5*

Lord, if it means that I can become whole again, keep me close to the floor, where my inability to speak allows You unhindered access to my heart.

SUFFERING WITH GRACE

━━━━ ━━━ ━━━━

The chief pang of most trials is not so much the actual
suffering itself as our own spirit of resistance to it.

JEAN-NICHOLAS GROU

As I was beginning to write about suffering, I heard on the news that missionary Martin Burnham had been killed during an attempt to rescue him and his wife, Gracia, who had been held hostage by Muslim extremists for more than a year. The couple had been vacationing at a resort in the Philippines, celebrating their eighteenth wedding anniversary, when they were taken captive in 2001.

Now, I don't know much about the Burnhams' specific work as missionaries, because the publicity understandably centered on their captivity. But I'm going to go out on a limb here and assume that they faced monumental hardships and challenges in their work. In many ways, a foreign missionary is the very definition of a misfit, a stranger in a strange land. I suspect there were times when they experienced a fair degree of suffering in their work, whether that suffering was physical, emotional, or even spiritual. I can only imagine how much they looked forward to their anniversary trip.

For the next year, they faced unimaginable circumstances. They watched their captors kill other hostages and never knew from one day to the next when their number would come up. Separated from their children, they must have despaired over the agony their family and loved ones were suffering on their behalf. Both became physically debilitated. And then, when hope was finally in sight, Martin was killed anyway.

If anyone living today has a reason to ask "Why me, God?" it's Gracia Burnham. According to the initial interviews, however, that was not what she did. Neither Martin nor Gracia seemed to have asked that question. Instead of resisting—and placing their fellow captives in jeopardy—they accepted their captivity with all its hardships, doing what they could to stay alive while learning to love their enemies. That's a tall order.

By comparison, most of us have suffered far less trauma and heartache, and yet we ask that question of God when even minor problems occur in our lives. In saying that, I'm not diminishing the pain and suffering that others—maybe even you—may be experiencing. The problem is that we often ask the question with such astonishment and dismay. But suffering should never come as a surprise to those of us who have a relationship with Christ. The Gospels and the Epistles warn us to expect persecution and trials, and yet when they come, we try to pray them away and command them to leave, seldom thinking that maybe God is up to something more significant than our suffering will ever amount to.

That is, after all, what He was up to as Jesus suffered on the cross—something much bigger than the disciples could see as they agonized over the death of their leader. Somehow, the Burnhams were able to see what the disciples could not, that they were part of a "something bigger" that God intended to accomplish in the Philippines. I suspect there's a fair-to-middling chance that He's using your suffering in a more significant way as well.

Resisting a trial, like resisting the very nature God has given us, only makes the situation worse. As you learn to accept your misfit nature with grace, be aware of all those other situations that God is asking you to accept with an equal measure of grace.

∽

Dear friends, do not be surprised at the painful trial you are suffering,
as though something strange were happening to you.
1 Peter 4:12

———————————

Lord, even if I can't see Your purpose in the trials I experience, give
me the grace to accept the suffering and trust You with the outcome.

MISFIT PUNISHMENT

———

"I call myself The Misfit," he said, "because I can't
make what all I done wrong fit what all I gone
through in the punishment."

FLANNERY O'CONNOR

lannery O'Connor's Misfit was a low-down dirty dog, the last guy on earth you would want to run into if your car happened to break down on a desolate country road, which is exactly what happened to several other characters in O'Connor's story. He's the sort of misfit who would scare the daylights out of you, with good reason. The guy was a killer, but I can overlook that for the moment. His definition of a misfit rings true with me, and besides, he's not real.

Think about his definition with regard to your own life. What have you done that's so bad? Probably lots of things, but right now I mean only those things that were caused by your eccentric way of thinking. When you consider your quirky behavior against the punishment you've had to endure, it hardly seems like an equitable relationship. You may have been mocked, scorned, abandoned, rejected, and condemned by others. And look at what you've done to yourself—you've probably tried to make "right" what was never wrong to begin with, your true nature. Without a doubt, "all you done wrong don't fit what all you gone through in the punishment."

So what are you going to do to reverse that unbalanced ratio? You can start by refusing to punish yourself any longer. You can't make right what isn't wrong, so you might as well stop trying to behave in a way that is contrary to your God-given nature. You can also refuse to react to the petty forms of punishment that others love to inflict on you: the affected glances, the pitiful stares, the rolling eyes, the oh-so-subtle smirks. You can decide in advance that you will not let their predictable mockery get to you. (I've trained myself to react by thinking *My, how very mature* and then suppressing the overwhelming urge to countersmirk.)

The not-so-petty forms of punishment are another matter. Abandonment and rejection and condemnation cut to the core of your being and tempt you to second-guess your own self-worth. Few people can steel themselves against that kind of punishment without becoming hardened and bitter in the process, and that's not the kind of outcome you want. I know of no way to remain merciful and forgiving in the face of cruelty other than to rely on Jesus and identify with Him in His suffering. And I don't just mean His physical suffering on the last day of His earthly life. I mean all the mocking and rejection and abandonment He experienced in the final three years of His life, much of it from people He knew intimately, all of it from people He loved.

Use rejection by others to reaffirm God's acceptance of you. Use abandonment to remind yourself that Jesus will never, ever abandon you. And use the condemnation of others as an opportunity to thank God that because of Jesus Christ, He will not condemn you.

Therefore, there is now no condemnation for those who are in Christ Jesus, because through Christ Jesus the law of the Spirit of life set me free from the law of sin and death.

Romans 8:1–2

Father, thank You for promising never to reject me or abandon me or condemn me. Keep me from punishing myself and taking on the punishment others try to inflict on me.

"THE HORROR! THE HORROR!"

You will never find Jesus so precious as when the world is one vast howling wilderness. Then he is like a rose blooming in the midst of the desolation, a rock rising above the storm.

ROBERT MURRAY MCCHEYNE

For most of us, the world became one vast howling wilderness on September 11, 2001, and the days following. We sat in stunned silence, transfixed by scenes of desolation, the aftermath of a cruel human storm of incomprehensible magnitude. We needed Jesus. We needed Him now.

Even in the first hour, I wondered how anyone would get through that day without the peace and strength that comes from knowing Him. I tried to put myself in the position of any of the women whose husband or fiancé or child was in the World Trade Center or the Pentagon or aboard one of the doomed planes that day. I am certain my effort fell far short of their emotions, but this one fact was indisputable—surviving the horror without sensing the presence of God was unimaginable. I became like Joseph Conrad's Mr. Kurtz in *Heart of Darkness*, able only to utter two words—"The horror! The horror!"—as the life flowed out of him. The horror rendered me nearly speechless.

But slowly, glimpses of Jesus began to emerge. In the people who stood ready to comfort those who arrived at the attack sites to wait and grieve and hope long after hope was gone. In the cross-shaped steel girders that rose from the ashes of the World Trade Center. In the courage of a handful of passengers on a flight over Pennsylvania who sacrificed their own lives so countless others would be saved.

In the months since, we've gotten on with our lives, those of us who were one step removed from direct involvement with the horror. And we think we're OK. But many of us have internalized the horror, and the world has become one vast howling wilderness within. Once again, we need Jesus, and we need Him now. Unlike the situation on September 11, though, we may not realize it—or admit it.

People who have never had an encounter with Jesus find this impossible to comprehend. How can a man who lived two thousand years ago, no matter how special He was, ever minister to people alive today? How can anyone say that He ministered to them in the aftermath of September 11? Answering those questions in a way that will make sense to one who has not had that encounter is like trying to "smell the color nine," as Christian songwriter Chris Rice describes the mystery of God. It can't be done. But leading that wondering soul into her own encounter with Jesus, well, that's another matter altogether, and one that can be done.

You can show others the rose that you see blooming amid the desolation, whether that desolation is visible like the hole left in the earth where the twin towers once stood, or whether it's invisible, like the hole left in a person's life when they've lost someone they love. And you can lead others to the Rock that you see rising above the storm, providing them with a safe and unshakable foundation that no howling wind or raging sea can demolish.

People who see things that other people cannot see, things that provide comfort and shelter and strength, are in a unique position to lead others to safety in the midst of the horrors of life. You are one of those people. Like those who led others to safety only to lose their own lives, you have no guarantee that you will emerge unscathed. As a Christian, though, you will ultimately emerge in a better place. That's what saving lives is about—and we have Jesus as proof.

For in the day of trouble
he will keep me safe in his dwelling;
he will hide me in the shelter of his tabernacle
and set me high upon a rock.
Psalm 27:5

Lord, grant me the strength and courage to lead others to safety
when I can clearly see the safe haven that remains hidden to them.

LIVING ON THE FRINGE

Read, every day, something no one else is reading.
Think, every day, something no one else is thinking. Do, every day,
something no one else would be silly enough to do. It is bad for
the mind to continually be part of unanimity.

CHRISTOPHER MORLEY

*M*aybe you've heard of Simon Stylites. He was a singular fifth-century character who got his name entered into the religious history books because of
the extreme measures he took to prove his devotion to God. He once wrapped a
rope around his body so tightly that he nearly died—not from asphyxiation, but
from the wounds that festered on his skin. Apparently unsatisfied with that
effort, he went on a forty-day Lenten fast—abstaining from food *and* water. After
cheating death a second time, he retreated to a mountainside, where he lived
out in the open, dressed in the skins of wild animals—and chained to a rock.

He is most remembered, however, for his final effort, the one that gave him
a last name, so to speak. Constantly visited by people who believed that a touch
from this holy man would heal them, Simon built a ten-foot-high *stylos*, or pillar, to avoid being besieged by the crowd. Over the next thirty-seven years—the

final years of his life—he was forced to increase the height of his pillar until it reached seventy feet. From a platform on top, he preached and prayed, seldom taking a break.

Misfits tend to live on the fringes of society, but few have lived quite as far out there as Simon did. From a distance of fifteen hundred years, we're likely to look on his behavior as quaint or primitive. Ascetics and hermits dotted the countryside in Simon's day, living in caves and dispensing their spiritual wisdom to the occasional visitor, so although Simon was more eccentric than most desert dwellers, he was certainly not alone.

But he had guts, the guts to live the way he thought he was supposed to, regardless of what anyone else believed about his ability to accurately hear God. Put yourself in Simon's place. Imagine being as close to sane as you've ever been and suddenly sensing that you should do something that no one else would be silly enough to do. Imagine, too, that you know that this prompting to do something bizarre came straight from God. Would you have the guts to obey?

Unless I was in a particularly cantankerous, society-hates-me-anyway frame of mind, I'd probably start modifying that bizarre something. I'd start to rationalize: *Haven't I heard a bunch of preachers say that it's our* willingness *to obey that matters with God?* Like Abraham holding a knife above the sacrificial body of his son Isaac, I would proudly show God my willingness. Naturally, I have the benefit of knowing how the Isaac story ended, so I would walk away feeling confident that I had done just what God required—although no more. So God, You want me to build a seventy-foot-high platform in my back yard and live up there and preach and pray? I'd be glad to. But of course, the city will never approve the necessary permits, so we'll just call it a draw. But Lord, I sure was willing!

Sometimes, whether we like it or not, we're called to do things that make us appear even more strange than usual. It's not a whole lot of fun, but we can't let the judgment of others interfere with our obedience to God. World-changers generally don't have minds that conform to unanimous opinion anyway. In the end, there's only One whose opinion matters.

We have different gifts, according to the grace given us.
Romans 12:6a

Lord, never let me allow the opinions of others to prevent me from obeying You, no matter how strange Your assignment may appear to be.

TURNING ODDITIES
INTO OPPORTUNITIES

I do not believe anyone ever yet humbly, genuinely,
thoroughly gave himself to Christ without some other
finding Christ through him.

PHILLIPS BROOKS

One of the questions I long to ask the Lord is what makes Him think He can use me to help usher in the kingdom of God. Really, in church we're told over and over just how important each believer is in God's plan of redemption, but no one has yet explained to me how someone as off-kilter as I am can possibly be a vital part of that plan. Sure, I've led people to the Lord, but I just figure that every now and then God's compassion gets the better of Him, and He starts to feel sorry for me. So He hands over someone who's ripe for the picking anyway, and we pray together, and the person gets saved, and everybody ends up satisfied, if not certifiably happy.

If you're as hard on yourself as I am, you know what I'm talking about. You get this uneasy feeling that no one could ever really see Jesus in you, and if they did, you'd start to worry about their image of Jesus. Obviously, any normal person would develop an immediate inferiority complex if someone said they could see Jesus in him. But I'm talking about the notion that a person would perceive Jesus as being eccentric like me. It's a scary thought.

This would be why I believe in the incomparable power of the Holy Spirit. Has it ever occurred to you, as it has to me, that the Holy Spirit does all kinds of transformational things with your words and your actions? At times, I've had people thank me for giving them wise counsel when I know full well that I had no clue what I was talking about and may not even remember the conversation at all. I'm convinced I've said something like "blah-blah-blah-blah" to some needy soul, and the Holy Spirit has come along, pulled my words out of the air, breathed on them, and turned them into "We are all pencils in the hand of a writing God, who is sending love letters to the world." So I get credit for something Mother Teresa said, but the needy soul feels uplifted, and the Holy Spirit has saved the day once again.

That's also why I think Phillips Brooks is probably right in saying that even a stammering fool can show Christ to another person if that fool is given over to God. That's not verbatim, but it's close enough to what he meant. And I know Jesus is right in saying that people will know we're His disciples if we love one another, because (1) He's Jesus, and He's always right; and (2) I've seen it happen. Christians are never better than they are in a crisis, which may be why we have so many; God knows that most believers are great at providing love and practical care in an emergency. And then there are the few that show the love of Jesus all the time, taking up the slack that the rest of us have created.

It's probably safe to say that you don't have to worry about how your oddities will play in the witnessing arena. The Holy Spirit is able—and believe me, more than willing—to turn your idiosyncrasies into opportunities to usher in the kingdom of God, even if the only words you speak sound like "blah-blah-blah-blah."

෧෧

"A new command I give you: Love one another. As I have loved you, so you must love one another. By this all men will know that you are my disciples, if you love one another."

John 13:34–35

Lord, thank You for sending the Holy Spirit to rescue me and my kind from our inadequate selves. Let me never forget that You alone are my adequacy.

NO ILLUSIONS

God is not disillusioned with us.
He never had any illusions to begin with.

LUIS PALAU

I spent much of my early life as a Christian believing that I was this great big disappointment to God. How could I not feel that way? From just about the very moment I came into a vital relationship with Jesus, Christians who seemed to know a whole lot more about the way God operates started giving me advice ("You really should go to Bible college, you know") or making prophetic statements about my future ("I just know God has a place for you in Campus Crusade for Christ!"). I was young, I was impressionable, and I was determined to please God. I came to believe that if I would follow the predictable path for a college-age believer in the early 1970s, that would make God very happy.

Not one thing in my life went according to this prescribed plan. I earned my degree at a private secular college and went to work at a daily newspaper. Although lots of Christians pointed out how important my job at the newspaper was, they often added a postscript: "Really, it's just as important as full-time Christian work." They made it sound as if I had missed the boat—*the* boat. But oh well, another one came along that appeared to be just as seaworthy. And in reality, I was OK with that until fifteen or so years later when a serious bout with postpartum depression convinced me that I had not fulfilled the promise that I had once shown. I hadn't exactly set the world on fire, evangelistically speaking, and now I wasn't even working as religion editor. And of course, a lot of Christians pointed out how important my job as a mother was, but they often added a postscript to that as well: "Besides, you can go back to work as soon as your kids go to school!" They made it seem as if I was now two steps removed from God's best. Well, how could God not be disappointed in me?

Today I know enough about chronic depression to understand how this first brief taste of it warped my thinking. I don't want to make light of it, but I have to admit—I was a pretty pathetic creature. Just how much of God's eternal plan did I think He had entrusted to me and me alone? What made me think that God expected anything more from me than He got? Furthermore, what made me think I had to follow some prescribed course in order to please Him? All He ever wanted was for me to have reverence for Him, walk in His ways, love Him with all my heart and soul, and observe His commandments (Deuteronomy 10:19). He never told me to do the "expected" thing; on the contrary, He showed Himself to be the God of the unexpected. The "unexpected," as it turned out, applied to my life as well.

If you feel you've been this great big disappointment to God, remember— He has never had any illusions about you or anyone else who ever lived. He may know your limitations, but He also knows your heart. He may know where you strayed from His will, but He also sees where you got back on track. He may know your potential, but He also sees—far better than you ever will—how close you've come to meeting it. Who knows? Maybe you've already exceeded it.

But Jesus would not entrust himself to them, for he knew all men. He did not need man's testimony about man, for he knew what was in a man.

John 2:24–25

Father, thank You for sending Jesus to earth to live like one of us. May we never doubt that You understand our humanity and love us in spite of it.

THE LIFE YOU WERE MADE FOR

Think of times in your life that made you wish for all the
world that you had the power to make time stand still. . . .
Something in your heart says, Finally—it has come.
This is what I was made for!

JOHN ELDREDGE

ohn Eldredge is one of those wonderful people who dares to shake up the
status quo by challenging some of society's most treasured assumptions. Like
this one: Life is not a dress rehearsal. *Oh, really?* Eldredge asks. *It most certainly
is,* he counters. God is shaping us now for the full performance to come in the
next life, the real life. And He is continually calling us up into the larger story of
this life, though most of us are so preoccupied with our own little stories that we
fail to hear His call.

Once in a while, though, His beckoning breaks through. It's at those
moments that we wish we could make time stand still; our heart recognizes
some aspect of our life's dream that we have neglected in our duty-filled lives,
and we want to savor it for as long as we can. Every one of those moments in my
life has occurred in the mountains. One evening in particular, as my husband

and I watched the sun set over Luray, Virginia, after a day of backpacking on the Appalachian Trail, I remember thinking, *I could die right now and feel as if my life has been complete.* And I was only in my early thirties. But I had been called up into a scene that was part of a larger story, through which God allowed me to catch a glimpse of the spiritual reality to come. In that scene, that evening, He became for me the peace that passes understanding.

Those moments of breakthrough are a gift. They come unbidden from a God who wants us to recognize our desire for "life as it was meant to be," in Eldredge's words, the life we lost when we lost Eden. But why does God allow those moments to surface? Why does He give us a longing for something we've lost, something we can never regain this side of heaven? At times, I've dismissed that longing as idealistic and impractical; I believed my intense desire for an idyllic life was yet another quirk that set me apart from normal people. But it turned out that the longing was yet another aspect of my nature that God wanted me to acknowledge and accept. Not to torment me but to keep me from losing heart.

Part of the purpose for that sense of longing, of course, is to keep before you the longing that you as a Christian should have for heaven. There's a more immediate purpose, though, and that's to give you a life worth living in the here and now. Once you learn to treasure them, those times of wonder and pure bliss allow you to become fully alive. Finally, it comes—the life you were meant to live, if only for a moment. But sometimes, a moment is enough.

တ

> Those living far away fear your wonders;
> where morning dawns and evening fades
> you call forth songs of joy.
>
> *Psalm 65:8*

Lord, give me the grace to not lose heart. Keep me from getting so accustomed to my duty-filled life that I lose the longing for life as You intended it to be.

BREATHING DEEPLY IN FAITH

Teach me, O God, not to torture myself, not to make a martyr out of myself through stifling reflection, but rather teach me to breathe deeply in faith.

SØREN KIERKEGAARD

It's been years since I studied Kierkegaard, and when I did, I had no personal interest in his approach to faith. For all I know, some of his religious beliefs may be off the mark, but this much I remember: He was an odd bird. A hopeless overthinker, he was subject to excessive brooding and bouts with depression. He's the kind of guy that would provoke you to rationalize away verses like Romans 12:15; mourning with someone like him would be tantamount to begging for a long hospital stay.

At least he recognized his tendency to torture himself, and he sought relief. He understood that his "stifling reflection" was suffocating him and feeding his martyr complex. Now, I'm not saying that I can relate to all that on a personal level. My interest in his oppressive nature is purely academic. But for argument's sake, I'll pretend.

What I'm sure I would have learned once I began to suffocate from pathetic self-absorption is the monumental difference between unhealthy introspection and divinely directed self-reflection. The former could prove deadly for those of us who believe we are among society's outcasts; the latter allows God to shine His light of revelation into our lives to give us a deeper understanding of the nature He placed within us. His light enables us to let go of our woe-is-me tendency toward martyrdom and replaces it with an openness to see and accept ourselves as we are.

And then comes the payoff, learning to "breathe deeply in faith." That's a great phrase to keep accessible throughout the day, every day. Breathing is an unusual function of the body, because it's both involuntary and voluntary. In other words, most of the time, you breathe without thinking, but sometimes you are consciously in control of the breaths you take. I'm guessing Kierkegaard the thinker realized how that dual aspect of physical breathing could also apply to breathing in faith. The faith that we breathe in on a regular basis—assuming we're in relationship with God—is akin to our involuntary breathing. It's usually on the shallow side but absolutely critical to keeping us alive. When we breathe deeply in faith, though, we are consciously in control; our attention is turned to our need to breathe deeply, intentionally drawing on more of the "breath of heaven," the Holy Spirit, who gives life to our faith.

What a contrast there is between torturous, suffocating introspection and deep life-filled breathing. Anxiety begins to slip away as we turn our focus from ourselves to the Spirit of God. As we seek relief, God's consolation—His comfort and encouragement—leaves us with little justification to continue our brooding.

Not that I would know any of this from personal experience. It's just an educated guess.

∞

When anxiety was great within me,
your consolation brought joy to my soul.
Psalm 94:19

———————————————

Lord, when my anxious thoughts multiply within me, Your encouraging comfort brings delight to my soul. Remind me throughout the day to breathe in Your life-giving faith.

RECKLESS ABANDON TO GOD

Never make a principle out of your experience; let God be as original with other people as He is with you.

OSWALD CHAMBERS

A while back, I spent several years hanging around the edges of a particular revival movement. It doesn't matter which one, because they're all essentially the same despite their differences: The Spirit manifests Himself in a certain manner, shaking things up a bit, and then the Spirit changes the way He operates. Somehow, the leadership doesn't always get this, so they keep the revival propped up long after the Spirit has altered the program, and anyone who begins to head off in a different direction ranks maybe one rung higher than an infidel.

When I began to step away from this particular movement—which was not a long walk to begin with—the diehards started in on me: "What about the move of God? How can you walk away like that?" Pretty easily, as it turned out, because God was leading me in such a different direction that to remain where I was would have amounted to an act of defiance. The diehards had turned their experience into a principle, their own personal doctrine. Without realizing it, they were trying to prevent God from being as original with me as He had been with them.

I don't blame them, really. When you've seen God work in a powerful way, it's difficult to keep a balanced perspective. I imagine the blind man of Bethsaida in Mark 8 faced some momentary temptation to turn his healing experience into a doctrine; from his perspective, sight would be restored if Jesus spit on your eyes. That indeed was an original method of healing, one that Jesus used on only three recorded occasions. Had He done that today, some marketing genius undoubtedly would have tried to turn it into a product, not a principle and not a pleasant thought.

I confess that I've been guilty of expecting God to work in someone else's life the way He worked in mine. I suppose that's understandable; it's all too easy to feel threatened by God's originality with others. If God is telling my friend to chuck it all and head for the mission field because the time is growing short, then I've got to wonder why He's telling me to stay put. Or if people are getting healed all over the place at some wild charismatic meetings, I wonder if He's really leading me to a time of contemplative prayer as I battle the flu. I'm sure I would feel a whole lot more secure if I could get my friend to stay home from the mission field and convince the charismatics to contemplate their way to healing. It has always come as a shock when I've realized that God's main concern is not making sure I feel secure.

Originality is what keeps us on the fringes, but it's also what we need to fight for. And we can't very well do that if we're undermining God's unique activity in another person's life. If we feel called to serve God with "reckless abandon"—another Oswald Chambers phrase—we need to give our fellow believers the freedom to do the same. Our artificially manufactured principles can only get in their way.

Accept one another, then, just as Christ accepted you, in order to bring praise to God.

Romans 15:7

Lord, let me be recklessly abandoned to You, allowing You to be original not only with me but also with those whose calling bears the marks of Your unique touch.

THE SWEET PAIN OF LONELINESS

*The awareness of loneliness might be a gift we must protect
and guard, because our loneliness reveals to us an inner emptiness
that can be destructive when misunderstood, but filled with
promise for him who can tolerate its sweet pain.*

HENRI J. M. NOUWEN

I've never thought of myself as a cruise type of person. My idea of a great vacation involves mountains and canyons and babbling brooks, and not the kind Carnival might be tempted to create on its promenade decks. But if I had known about Henri Nouwen back when he was a cruise line chaplain, I might have forked over six months' pay to join his ship on a transatlantic jaunt. I wouldn't even have needed to feign a spiritual crisis as an excuse to seek him out for counseling, because throughout my life, I've regularly had some spiritual crisis or other going. I'd just have to make sure it reached its critical stage shortly after embarkation. I would want to sit at the feet of this spiritual giant for as long as possible.

Nouwen's writings were seldom better than when he lent his thoughtful insight to the painful emotional issues people face every day—like loneliness.

And although his cruise-line job amounted to little more than a footnote to the rest of his career, he must have seen his share of lonely people aboard those cruise ships. With their promise of round-the-clock entertainment and activities, cruises symbolize our misguided notion that nonstop "doing" can fill up the lonely places in our soul. At best, all that activity merely postpones our next inevitable confrontation with loneliness. At worst, it magnifies the hollowness inside to a frightening degree.

Nouwen came to recognize the "sweet pain" of loneliness as a precious gift that invites us to look beyond our limited horizons and become "wounded healers"—those who minister to the lonely in our midst even as we try to come to grips with our own loneliness. He compares the wound of loneliness to the Grand Canyon—a deep incision that is also an inexhaustible source of beauty. It's the type of beauty, though, that we need to drink in and explore. Like the rushed tourist who spends a few hours at the Grand Canyon before heading to the next attraction, many of us seldom take the time to wander along the hidden pathways to discover the beauty that lies within our own feelings of emptiness.

Loneliness, I've come to realize, is not something that can be resisted with any degree of success. The more you feel alienated from society, the more loneliness you will experience—not exactly good news for misfits, unless you are willing to enter into loneliness and discover its beauty, its sweet pain. Instead of running off to the next "attraction"—whatever form your time-consuming busyness takes—staying put could be the best form of therapy when that empty feeling begins to unnerve you. As you mentally follow the hidden pathways in your soul, you will likely begin to understand some of the reasons why a loving God would let you continue to feel so lonely for so long. And that kind of therapy costs a whole lot less than a transatlantic cruise.

But Jesus often withdrew to lonely places and prayed.
Luke 5:16

Lord, show me what You want me to learn through the loneliness in my life, keeping me always mindful of the truth that the only permanent cure for the emptiness inside is being in Your presence.

MISFIT SAINTS

━━━━ ■ ━━ ■ ━━━━

*A saint has to be a misfit. A person who embodies what his culture
considers typical or normal cannot be exemplary.*

MARTIN MARTY

I f you ever start to feel sorry for yourself because of your alienation from normal society, you can take heart in the realization that virtually every world-
changer, whether for good (Jesus, of course) or for bad (Hitler, of course), was a
misfit. Those who have no influence on the world are those who adhere to the
status quo—precisely because they want it to remain the status quo. As theolo-
gian and church scholar Martin Marty pointed out, in order for a person's life to
be exemplary, he or she has to stand apart as different. Saints symbolize the best
of both scenarios: They are exemplary, and they are world-changers.

One of the best-known world-changing, beatified misfits was St. Francis of
Assisi. If your knowledge of Francis is limited to the current crop of garden stat-
uary that honors the saint's affinity for God's creatures, you might want to know
a few other choice tidbits about him. Yes, it's apparently true that birds ate right
out of his hand; hence, the birdfeeder Francis. But it's also true that following

his conversion as a young man, he took the Bible so literally that he based the remainder of his life on three verses chosen at random one day. Forsaking his family's wealth—which Francis had copiously availed himself of as a youth—he gave away everything he owned, acquired a rough woolen shepherd's tunic, and began to preach publicly. Despite his odd appearance—or perhaps because of it—he attracted a significant following. His commitment to poverty astonished both society and the church; his identification with the poor empowered his preaching.

Being different for the sake of being different gets you nowhere. But if it's your convictions that set you apart and possibly even lead you to a radical lifestyle change, then you've got something. If your distinctiveness does not serve a larger purpose, it's mere ornamentation; if a radical lifestyle change does not flow from a call and a conviction, it will be ineffective—both in your own life and in the lives of those people that God wants you to influence.

You can't make yourself different in order to change society; God is the one who made you different, and it's within that uniqueness that you can effect change. What kind of change? You may not ever know; Francis certainly didn't. He could not have known that the movement he started would influence countless people over hundreds of years. Like Francis, you can start to be a society-rattling influence through your willingness to be a radical believer. You may not end up being a world-changer, but then again, you never know.

∞

Blessed are you when men hate you, when they exclude you and insult you and reject your name as evil, because of the Son of Man. Rejoice in that day and leap for joy, because great is your reward in heaven. For that is how their fathers treated the prophets.

Luke 6:22–23

Lord, grant me the courage to be so completely sold out to You that I will obey Your most radical intention for my life, without ever looking back.

CHURCH LIFE AS A LAB RAT

I wish they would remember that the charge to Peter was
"Feed my sheep," not "Try experiments on my rats," or even
"Teach my performing dogs new tricks."

C. S. LEWIS

f I were challenged to come up with the name of my literary hero, it would be a formidable task. I think, though, that I would eventually have to settle on C. S. Lewis, who handled words with precision and dexterity. If he ever wrote a bad sentence, I haven't read it. And if you have, please don't feel the need to pass your knowledge along to me. Sometimes ignorance truly is bliss.

With regard to faith—or in this case, the church—Lewis is my spiritual soul mate. In the opening of *Letters to Malcolm*, the source of the quote above, he maintains that innovation in church services transfers the focus from God to the innovation. I'm more flexible than Lewis, but I understand his point. These days, the praise and worship time in independent churches often turns into a concert performance as the worship team goes off on its own, leaving the congregation stranded. The people in the seats end up forgetting all about God as they try to figure out what is going on up front. Then again, if I had to look out over a lethargic congregation week after week, even I might be tempted to put on some kind of eye-opening show.

But as a layperson, I'm tired of being experimented on. I spent years in churches where the leadership changed its focus and direction every six months or so. You'd no sooner get used to one program than they'd change it on you. As a result, your attention would be on adjusting to the change and not on worshiping Jesus.

Where does that leave you if you're involved in one of those ever changing churches? Obviously you could go to another church, and of course you should pray for the leaders. But maybe you feel compelled to stay. What then? If you're already suspect because you're a misfit, you might as well go whole hog and find your own way of worship in the midst of all this entertainment. That may mean getting to church early enough to sit quietly and focus all of your attention on Jesus, no matter what is going on around you. It may also mean tuning out some of the service and continuing your interior conversation with the Lord. And you may have to refuse to participate when you feel uncomfortable with a particular innovation—like shoulder massaging, designed to break the ice and show your neighbor you care. I guess I don't care, because I've decided I'll be the one to determine who gets to touch me and when.

To go along with an innovation or activity that is contrary to your way of thinking is often much worse than having everyone look at you because you chose to sit it out. You only have to put up with their stares for a few minutes, but you have to live with yourself twenty-four hours a day. And you probably don't want to go through those hours feeling like a performing dog or a laboratory rat.

෨෧

Do not lord it over those in your charge, but be examples to the flock.
1 Peter 5:3 (NRSV)

———————————————

Father, let me be so sensitive to Your Spirit that I will be able to immediately discern when I'm being true to my convictions and when I'm just being obstinate. Let my motives always be pure and right in Your sight.

A BRAND-NEW ENDING

Though no one can go back and make a brand-new start,
anyone can start from now and make a brand-new ending.

CARL BARD

For someone with as many regrets in life as I have, Carl Bard's words are a source of comfort and strength. Just because I got off on the wrong foot, he assures me, that doesn't mean that I have to keep hopping on that same foot. I can shift to the other foot and make a brand-new ending for my life. Not a bad deal at all.

Among evangelicals, believers often joke about their "B.C." lives—their lives before Christ. I did the same, without realizing how deeply that kind of thinking colored my attitude toward life. Certainly, everything changed the day I was saved, and the change has continued in the nearly thirty years since then. But by focusing so much on that demarcation, I was ignoring another demarcation, the one that comes with the dawning of each new day. My twisted mind separated sin into B.C. and P.S.—postsalvation. I had no problem believing that the sins, mistakes, and general foul-ups in my B.C. phase were washed away by the blood of Christ. But I tended to look at those in my P.S. life as something of a postscript: "And she kept on sinning, until the day she died." Well, of course I did. But that didn't mean that my life couldn't change just as dramatically today, or any day, as it did thirty years ago.

So I'm learning to start from now and make a brand-new ending for my life. The daily offices of the Episcopal liturgy keep me grounded in this effort, but maybe I just need more structure than other people do. I'm thinking there are probably about as many ways to make a brand-new ending as there are people on earth. Your way may be completely unstructured but just as effective as mine, in which case I envy you. But envy is a topic for another week.

Your future is never set in stone, no matter what you think. Look around at the people you know whose lives have been dramatically and unexpectedly changed. I often think of a young woman I knew who had six children, all by her husband, a man who espoused the sanctity of marriage and apparently chose 1 Timothy 2:15 as his life verse ("But women will be saved through childbearing and by continuing to live in faith, love, holiness, and modesty"). He made sure she was good and saved, but then he divorced her. Everyone pronounced doom and gloom on her future chances for remarriage; what man in his right mind would take on such a huge responsibility? And yet an incredibly kind and loving man came along, fell in love with her and her children, and has spent the last fifteen years completely devoted to making their lives both full and joyful.

Never, ever let anyone try to convince you that you cannot experience a

brand-new ending to your life. God is faithful, and His "mercies begin afresh"
E.D.—each day.

଼୨

> The unfailing love of the LORD never ends! By his mercies we have
> been kept from complete destruction. Great is his faithfulness; his
> mercies begin afresh each day.
>
> *Lamentations 3:22–23 (NLT)*

Lord, I want a brand-new ending for my life. Daily remind me of Your
fresh mercies, Your unfailing love, and Your great faithfulness.

SANCTUARIES FOR YOUR SPIRIT

*Everybody needs beauty as well as bread, places to play in
and pray in, where nature may heal and cheer and give
strength to body and soul alike.*

JOHN MUIR

One of my favorite places in the country is the Red Canyon near South Pass City, Wyoming, a ghost town that was once a vibrant mining community. Red Canyon is not an especially dramatic site as canyons go. It's not all that deep, and to some people, I'm sure, it's not all that pretty. But it's the kind of place where I could sit on a rise for hours and do nothing but look out over the barren landscape. When I do—which is nowhere near often enough—my thoughts wander all over the map, from imagining the various land shifts and upheavals that formed each stratum in the ground, to wondering what the pioneers thought when they first spied the area, to praying a silent thank-you to God for allowing me to be there, to creating a classic cowboys 'n' Indians skirmish that would rival any in a 1950s western.

It doesn't make a bit of difference what I think about as I sit there; that site and others like it always become a worship sanctuary for my spirit. There, in the indescribable emptiness and silence of the landscape, God's presence is nearly palpable to me. I leave feeling healed and cheered and strengthened, and I carry with me a memory I can draw on when my everyday Florida life feels empty and silent.

At times, I find myself wondering what God was thinking when He created such an incredible array of environments. I'd like to believe that He was thinking ahead to His human creation and the need He knew we would have for natural sanctuaries for our spirit. A small clearing in a forest of lodgepole pines, a smooth and flat granite rock perfectly placed near a waterfall, a clump of sea oats on an oceanside sand dune—all become open-air cathedrals for our spirit. Even in cities where bulldozers have removed much of the evidence of God's original creation, the need for a natural sanctuary is obvious in city parks and tiny courtyard gardens.

If you can't remember the last time you visited such a sanctuary, it's probably time for a change in your routine. No matter where you live, a natural chapel isn't far away. Give yourself permission to take off a few hours for some quiet reflection and meditation amid the wonders of God's creation. Psalm 23 illustrates one of the results: "He makes me lie down in green pastures; he leads me beside still waters; he restores my soul" (verses 2–3a, NRSV). David was clearly aware of the link between the restoration of his soul and the natural world.

It's all too easy to put off the simple but restorative pleasures in our everyday lives. We think we can wait until our next vacation, until the next project is wrapped up, or until the season changes. But then vacation becomes another project, and the seasons keep changing, and we still haven't satisfied our soul's need to connect with God in the world He created without our help. Make a date with yourself to spend some time in that special sanctuary, the one that holds out the promise of healing and cheering and strengthening your body and soul alike.

> The heavens declare the glory of God;
> the skies proclaim the work of his hands.
> *Psalm 19:1*

Father, You went above and beyond all that I could have hoped for or imagined when You created a world filled with special sanctuaries for the spirit. Let me always be open to Your presence in Your creation.

THE SOUL ON ITS KNEES

Certain thoughts are prayers. There are moments when,
whatever be the attitude of the body, the soul is on its knees.

Victor Hugo

Sometimes I think my soul lives on its knees. Not because I'm so all-fired spiritual but because I'm so all-fired desperate. My soul has been on its knees for so long that I doubt it could stand up at this point, assuming that a soul could stand up in the first place. More overthinking, I know.

Maybe that's why I feel so drawn to contemplative prayer. My soul is already in position; all I need to do is turn my attention toward God. "In those moments of silence and peace when it pays no heed to what is happening within itself, [the soul] prays and prays excellently," wrote the eighteenth-century Jesuit priest Jean-Nicholas Grou in his classic work, *How to Pray*. Yes, that's it; that's what I sense when I engage in contemplative prayer. My soul is oblivious to what is happening, and it is praying excellently.

I don't exactly advertise my tendency toward contemplation, or at least I didn't until now. Some people already think I'm a space cadet, and those who misunderstand the nature of contemplative prayer tend to make jokes about mystical weirdos who do bizarre things like contemplate their navel. Though there may be some primordial symbolism connecting belly buttons and the divine, I could try to assure those people that I don't equate my navel with the nature of God, which is what I *am* contemplating. But why bother? My lack of concern about what other people think certainly does come in handy at times.

One of the drawbacks to contemplative prayer is the danger that we might equate our thoughts with our will. All of our silent reflection on God will prove meaningless if our will is not prepared to please God with our actions. That can be a scary proposition, and it's the fear of what God will require of us that too often keeps us from entering the deeper forms of prayer through which we allow God to do all the talking, should He choose to do so. Even though our will is submissive to our spirit when we pray, it must become engaged when God says it's time to get moving again.

If you've never practiced contemplative prayer, or realized that God might consider some of your thoughts to be prayer, you may find that this type of prayer suits your nature. Groups devoted to contemplative or "centering" prayer—in which a single word or phrase forms the focus of a set prayer time—meet throughout the country, and you can be sure you'll find a kindred soul or two there. If it weren't for misfits, such groups might not even exist. I suspect that your soul is already in position; it shouldn't take long at all for the other parts of you to catch up to it.

୭୭

In the same way, the Spirit helps us in our weakness. We do not know what we ought to pray for, but the Spirit himself intercedes for us with groans that words cannot express.

Romans 8:26

Lord, show me how to pray in a way that pleases You and ushers me into Your presence. Help me to quiet my thoughts and my spirit so You may be the focus of my prayer.

MORE OF GOD

The biggest human temptation is to settle for too little.

THOMAS MERTON

If you know anything about Thomas Merton, you know he is not talking about having it all in a material sense. Merton, a Trappist monk, put the Abbey of Gethsemani in Kentucky on the map after the publication of his best-selling autobiography, *The Seven Storey Mountain*, and spent the last seven years of his life in a hermitage on the monastery grounds. This was not a man whose life was dictated by the consumer mentality of contemporary America.

Merton was referring to our limited expectations of God. We pray and ask for certain things from God, and we're stunned when He actually comes through for us and gives us what we asked for. Maybe that's not such a bad thing, if it means we understand that God is not our servant, standing at attention just waiting to grant us every little desire of our heart. (If you ever need a reason to appreciate your life as it is today, meditate for a while on what your life would have been like if some genie in a bottle had actually granted your every little desire. You should be feeling better in no time.)

What Merton was getting at was not so much that we settle for less than He's willing to do for us; rather, we settle for less of God Himself than He wants to give us. He invites us to bask in His love; He beckons us to experience the wonder of His presence; He calls us to join Him in the glorious work of His kingdom. So what do we do? We go to church, and maybe pray and read the Bible, and if we're really serious, we go on a retreat once in a while. Meanwhile, God has got to be thinking, *What is wrong with these people?*

As Merton points out, what's wrong is that we've been tempted to settle for too little; we've gotten used to having less than God offers. We think that experiencing God's love and glory and presence and kingdom is for other people, like monks and ministers and missionaries, people in full-time ministry whose job description includes time alone with God. Or that it was available only to people who lived "back then," some mythical, simpler era in history when people had more time to enter into God's presence.

The reality is that people have always settled for less from God, and people have always filled up their time with things that distracted them from God — often out of necessity and not out of preference, as can be the case today. We complicate God right out of our lives and then wonder why we feel so empty.

Resist the temptation to settle for less of God than He wants you to have. You know where that temptation comes from; it's not from anyone who has your best intentions at heart, that's for sure. Resist the temptation, too, to look at the spiritual lives of others and feel that you must settle for what they have. Step away from the ordinary; seek the extraordinary from the Father, the one who longs to give you more.

Now to him who is able to do immeasurably more than all we ask or imagine, according to his power that is at work within us, to him be glory in the church and in Christ Jesus throughout all generations, for ever and ever! Amen.

Ephesians 3:20–21

God, I want more of You. I want all that You are holding out to me. I'm tired of settling for less. I believe You want me to experience the extraordinary.

WHY NOT ME?

━━━━━ ▭ ━━━━━

Sometimes I lie awake at night and ask, "Why me?"
Then a voice answers, "Nothing personal, your
name just happened to come up."

CHARLES SCHULTZ

One of my favorite *Peanuts* comic strips, long lost on a calendar circa 1971, showed Charlie Brown in musing mode, probably standing by Lucy's psychiatry stand. He asks something like, "Is it true that out of your entire life, one day will be better than all the rest?" In the second frame, ever logical Lucy assures him that the statement is indeed true. The third frame depicts a still-musing Charlie. "What if you've already had it?" he asks in defeat in the final frame.

Imagine being Charlie's age and having such a gloomy approach to the rest of your life. I did. Imagine it, that is, as that calendar page confronted me for an entire month. Schultz, I knew, had hit on something elemental in human nature, as he did with so many of his *Peanuts* strips. Like Charlie, at times I would wonder if the best had already passed; I wanted to return to a time when I was much younger than Charlie, in years and in spirit. Like Charlie, I seemed to have acquired an old soul at an early age.

Not long after that calendar year, I returned to the faith of my childhood, a belief in a personal God who loved me and cared about me. But once the blush of that new love had faded, I began asking the ultimate pity-party question: "Why me?" Why do I have to be the one to always accommodate other people, always forgive other people, always be nice to other people, for heaven's sake? Why do all these crummy things happen to me, and why do I have to always take it like a good little Christian? And why, oh why, did You make me so weird?

Twenty years ago, I might not have appreciated the answer Schultz got when he asked that question. Today, I not only love it, I believe it. My name just happened to come up. It was nothing personal, nothing intended to make my life miserable, nothing that would indicate that God loved me any less than the rest of humanity. My name just happened to come up. In other words, why not me?

If you've been asking God "Why me?" you're probably asking the wrong question. The way I see it these days, it matters very little why you and I are the way we are. Once we acknowledge that, the question becomes one for ourselves and not for God: OK, it does not matter why I'm this way. The question is, What am I going to do about it?

You are the only one who can give a satisfying answer to that. But you may have to ask a series of other questions before you do, like: What do I have to gain by resisting my true nature? Do I want to spend the rest of my life trying to change for the sake of some arbitrary definition of *normal?* What's the worst that could happen if I embraced my distinctions and lived an authentic life in harmony with them?

Sure, those questions are loaded, weighted in favor of being true to yourself. But you know what? Trying to be what you are not never gets any easier; it only gets more difficult and more frustrating. And you know what else? It's nothing personal. Your name just happened to come up, and it's a name God loves as much as any other.

૭૭

"I know that You can do everything
And that no purpose of Yours can be withheld from You.
You asked, 'Who is this who hides counsel without knowledge?'
Therefore I have uttered what I did not understand,
Things too wonderful for me, which I did not know."

Job 42:2–3 (NKJV)

Lord, show me what You want me to do about the nature You have placed within me—and keep reminding me not to take it out on You.

"I YAM WHAT I YAM"

I am not what I ought to be. I am not what I want to be.
I am not what I hope to be. But still, I am not what I used to be.
And by the grace of God, I am what I am.

JOHN NEWTON

When I read this quote from John Newton, who gave us the exquisite hymn "Amazing Grace," I couldn't help but hear Popeye's voice saying: "I yam what I yam and that's all that I yam!" Not what Newton had in mind, I grant you.

I never got to play the part of Popeye, one of the many bitter pills I had to swallow as a latter-born. My sister, the first-born of the brood still at home when Popeye was at his nautical peak, always got that choice role. My little brother landed the part of Popeye's nemesis and archenemy, Bluto, which I suppose was only fair because my brother was, of course, a boy. That left gangly and awkward me to be the gangly and awkward Olive Oyl, always stuck in the middle. The upside was that these two guys were always fighting over me. They weren't much to look at, but neither was I, so it all evened out in the end.

Today, I may not be all that I ought to be, want to be, or hope to be, but I am not what I used to be, and I don't mean the one who got stuck playing Olive Oyl all the time. I mean the one who got stuck for so many years trying to play a part that I was ill suited for. I am what I am, and the only part I'm suited to play is the role of Marcia Edwards and her subsequent name changes, ending with Ford. In that role, I'm a natural.

By the grace of God, you also are who you are today, and that means you are not what you used to be. Even if this whole faith experience is brand-new to you—or if you aren't sure you even believe in God yet—you are not what you used to be. The fact that you picked up this book, or any other book designed to help you see yourself in a different light, means that you are on the brink of change. You are no longer satisfied with what was. The same holds true for those who have been on a spiritual journey for years—or even decades. What used to be no longer satisfies.

Take your dissatisfaction and run with it. Get as far as you can from the role you've been trying to play, the one that makes you feel as if you are betraying your gut feeling about who you really are. A great Yiddish proverb expresses it like this: "If I try to be like him, who will be like me?" Only she can be like her; only you can be like you.

As with everyone else on the planet, you'll never be who you ought to be, want to be, or hope to be, but you can come awfully close by being who you are.

And thank God, that's not who you used to be.

◎

But by the grace of God I am what I am, and his grace to me was not without effect. No, I worked harder than all of them—yet not I, but the grace of God that was with me.

1 Corinthians 15:10

Father, I thank You for bringing me as far from my former self as You have. By Your grace, I pray that I will never again stray from my true self, the way You made me to be.

THE GOOD FIGHT

To be nobody but yourself in a world which is doing its best, night and day, to make you everybody else means to fight the hardest battle which any human being can fight, and never stop fighting.

E. E. CUMMINGS

No, E. E. Cummings did not always write his name in all lowercase letters, contrary to popular belief. And according to his widow, who ought to know these things, he did not have his name legally changed to lowercase style. As I find myself saying over and over again these days—so much for the legitimacy of popular belief.

But on to you. Are you ready for a fight? You need to be, because if you are an outsider, you are in for the fight of your life, for your life, for the rest of your life. Your fight, however, is not for a coveted place on the inside. Your fight is for your own place on the outside, on your own terms, in your own way.

No matter where I've worshiped or worked, people have always complained among themselves about the inner circle—those who had gained the special favor of the powers that be. They were the ones who formed the elite core, or corps, or corpse; all three words have proven to be accurate descriptions at various times and in different places. Sometimes I was one of the complainers, and sometimes I was perceived as being part of the inner circle, though I can assure you, that was an illusion. Most of the time, I was just out there on my own, not part of the inner circle or the outer circle. Where I was felt more like the outer limits.

And it was OK. It was more than OK, in fact. Because I gradually began to see that being accepted into the inner circle often meant losing bits and pieces of yourself. It meant having to express opinions that were not your own. It meant not only following the party line but having to preach it and recruit others to cross over to the accepted way of thinking. And it meant alienating—and often, nauseating—people like me, not that that would matter to anyone. (Is it any wonder that after exceedingly brief flirtations with both major political parties, I now register to vote as an independent?)

I like to think of the battle we're in as a skirmish in the larger "good fight" Paul referred to in his letters to Timothy. He encourages Timothy to "Fight the good fight of the faith. Take hold of the eternal life to which you were called when you made your good confession in the presence of many witnesses" (1 Timothy 6:12) and later mentions his own fight (2 Timothy 4:7). Your faith is at stake in this skirmish, by the way. If God is leading you in a different manner, then conforming to the accepted way of thinking may very well indicate a lack of faith that He will be with you as you face further ostracism. Like me, you probably know people who have been so wounded in battle that they have fallen away from the "good fight of faith" altogether.

Don't let that happen to you. Keep your eyes riveted to the Commander-in-Chief. If His generals try to give you alternative orders, just remember who you will answer to in the end.

I have fought the good fight, I have finished the race, I have kept
the faith.

2 Timothy 4:7

Lord, give me the grace and the strength to fight the good fight,
finish the race, and keep the faith, right to the end of my days on
earth.

INVISIBLE PEOPLE

*Let us treat men and women well; treat them as if
they were real. Perhaps they are.*

RALPH WALDO EMERSON

$\mathcal{H}$ ere in Florida, where I reluctantly live, we have what has to be one of the most incongruous demographic phenomena in the country: a highly visible population of invisible people. As a group, senior citizens are so prevalent in the state that they practically define Florida culture and lifestyle. As individuals, though, they are often ignored, ridiculed, or abused.

In one of its best series in recent years, the *Orlando Sentinel* drew attention to some of the individuals who are largely treated as part of a nameless, faceless mass of seniors by a younger population—and I'm defining *younger* as those under the age of 55. You can't blame this problem on Generation X alone. As I recall, the newspaper randomly chose elderly people to profile, and the treasures the reporters unearthed should have put many of their readers to shame. Yes, I was among the shamed. Even though I believe that every person has a story to tell, I don't always treat people that way. I treat them as if they aren't there, as if they aren't real.

What's so inexplicable about my behavior is that I know what it's like to be treated as if I were invisible. You've probably had similar experiences. Mine have usually taken place in church, when I've been face-to-face with a pastor, but only in a figurative sense. All too often, his face was turned away as he scanned the crowd for someone more important to talk to. And don't even get me started on the way Christian men treat my husband. In one church, he became known among my female friends as Snuffleupagus. Like Big Bird, I had my own invisible friend; the women—who could see what an incredible man I had somehow snagged—also saw how the men in the church treated him. He didn't fit in with their image of the typical Christian man, so they chose not to see him at all.

Several years ago at a cowboy church service held in a riding arena, the pastor dismounted his horse a few minutes before the service was to start. He approached me, extended his hand, and welcomed me to the service. I didn't instigate this. Trust me, I know better than to try to talk to a pastor right before or right after a service. I was just there, minding my own business, waiting for the service to begin. Someone had apparently pointed me out as a guest, and this cowboy decided I was worth greeting. He never took his eyes off me as we talked. Once he remounted his horse and started the service, it was all I could do to keep from crying. He had treated me as if I was real; it had been far too many years since a church leader had been that attentive and kind and interested in me as a person.

The ever entertaining G. K. Chesterton once maintained that there were no uninteresting things in the world, "only uninterested people." I'm tempted to add that there are no uninteresting people in the world, but having met my share of certifiable bores, I'll resist the temptation and offer a modified theory: No one's life story can remain boring when placed in the hands of a passionately interested person. Because everybody, even the most tiresome people you know, should be treated as if they are real. Because they are. No maybe about it.

> And you are to love those who are aliens, for you yourselves were aliens in Egypt.
>
> *Deuteronomy 10:19*

Lord, I want You to pull me up short whenever I treat other people as if they were invisible—and let me never forget how I feel when someone treats me that way.

A PROPER INSANITY

*No one is sane who does not know how to be insane
on proper occasions.*

HENRY WARD BEECHER

I must say, I do get a kick out of reading the Bible sometimes. Some parts are really funny, like the narration of the events in 1 Samuel 21. David has just found out for sure that King Saul is out to get him, so he starts seeking help wherever he can get it. He even goes to an enemy of Saul's, King Achish of Gath, but when he overhears the king's servants talking, he realizes he has made a mistake—the king has no intention of helping him. David figures the only way he can get out of this predicament alive is to pretend that he's insane, so he starts drooling and clawing. This was indeed a "proper occasion" calling for feigned insanity. What I especially like about the story, though, is Achish's response. "Am I so short of madmen that you have to bring this fellow here to carry on like this in front of me?" he asks incredulously. "Must this man come into my house?" (1 Samuel 21:15). The king is beset by imported insanity. I love it.

I'm assuming that's not the point of the story. I think we're given a fair warning here that there may come a time when we will have to decide whether we will risk our reputation to continue doing the work God has called us to do. David was not about to allow himself to be given over to the king to be killed. Seeing no other way out, he humiliated himself by acting completely out of his mind. It was a gamble, but it worked. If it hadn't, word surely would have spread throughout the region that Saul's relentless pursuit of David had caused him to come unglued. His success in escaping from Achish, however, eventually proved that his insanity was a ruse.

You could probably argue all day about whether he should have gone to King Achish in the first place, and I'm sure there are those who would take David to task for being deceptive. But I'm not about to play God in this situation; He may very well have led David to seek help from Achish and then act insane. Nothing, I've discovered, is beyond God. He is full of surprises.

But before we go proclaiming to all who will listen that yes, of course, we would risk our already shaky reputations for God, we need to remember that David had no guarantee that his ruse would work. Would we be willing to have others believe we are psychotic or deranged—or more peculiar than we actually are—for the sake of the kingdom of God?

For those of us who have had to work overtime to rebuild our reputation, this is not as easy a challenge as it seems. We may not be able to say with any certainty what we would do if we were in a predicament like David's. But this one thing I am able to say with certainty: The God to whom I entrusted my reputation—and everything else in my life—for all these years is the same God to whom I can entrust it all now and in the future. And operating within that trust is the only sane way I know to live.

David took these words to heart and was very much afraid of Achish king of Gath. So he pretended to be insane in their presence; and while he was in their hands he acted like a madman, making marks on the doors of the gate and letting saliva run down his beard.

1 Samuel 21:12–13

Father, make me always willing to risk everything—my life, my possessions, my name, my everything—for the sake of Your kingdom.

THE HOUND OF HEAVEN

I fled Him, down the labyrinthine ways
Of my own mind; and in the midst of tears
I hid from Him, and under running laughter.

FRANCIS THOMPSON

The college I attended housed its English department in Shadow Lawn, a magnificent mansion that once served as a summer White House for President Woodrow Wilson. If you saw the movie *Annie*, you saw the building. It was right there, in Daddy Warbucks's cinematic home, that I first read Francis Thompson's exquisite poem "The Hound of Heaven." Maybe I wouldn't have been as captivated by Thompson, or any other British or American poet, if it hadn't been for the grandeur of the aptly named Wilson Hall. Shelley and Whitman and Keats and Eliot and Thompson stand or fall on their own merits, of course, but it made for an extraordinary experience to read their poetry in a former ballroom, or even better, a former bedroom. One can only imagine.

A quick glance at the notes in the margins of my poetry anthology from the time verifies that we read a lot of religious verse that year. But no poem affected me quite the way Thompson's "Hound of Heaven" did. I felt as if I had been running right alongside Thompson as he tried to flee from God. But it seemed that the faster and farther I tried to run, the more ground He would gain on me, hounding me, nipping at my heels, sniffing my scent, flushing me out of my many hiding places. He never lost track of me, even as I zigged and zagged and weaved in and out of questionable places and situations.

Who knew? Who knew that this omnipresent God was in all those bars with me? Funny how I had managed to carry from my childhood the belief in a flesh-and-blood Adam and Eve but not in a God who meant it when He claimed to be everywhere. Even at the Student Prince and the Sunshine Inn and the Stone Pony, the Asbury Park clubs where Springsteen got his start, and at the no-name watering holes where no one seemed to start or finish but everyone seemed to just exist. God was there? I sure didn't think so. It's not as if He spoke to me or gave me any hint that He was hovering around. Or maybe He did.

In Psalm 139, David asks two rhetorical questions about the omnipresence of God, knowing full well the answer to all such questions: No matter where we go, God is there. For all our deft maneuvering, all our labyrinthine fleeing, all our shadowy hiding, we cannot shake Him. He remains on our trail, a faithful bloodhound dogging us at every turn.

Until finally, we give up. And we let Him take the lead.

Where can I go from your Spirit?
Where can I flee from your presence?
If I go up to the heavens, you are there;
if I make my bed in the depths, you are there.
Psalm 139:7–8

Lord, You hound me relentlessly and dog me at every turn. You just won't leave me alone. Thank You. And please, never, never stop.

AN UNTAMED FRONTIER

The spiritual life cannot be made suburban.
It is always frontier, and we who live in it must accept
and even rejoice that it remains untamed.

HOWARD MACY

Among the oddest items in the accumulated detritus I've saved in recent years is a Christian magazine that landed on my desk as a complimentary copy when I was working overtime and then some at another magazine. At the time, my daughters considered me their absentee mother, and I'm afraid to think of what my husband considered me to be.

The image on the cover caused me to recoil in disgust, which is why I saved it. Pretty images frustrate me; nauseating images inspire me in reverse. This was a nauseating image: A perfectly coiffed, perfectly dressed woman arrives home as a perfect grandfather clock strikes 9:30, several hours shy of what I would have considered a long day. She's carrying a briefcase (worker), a Bible (Christian), and a grocery bag brimming with obligatory fresh greens (model; the greens are too green, and no bagger arranges greens like that). Her teenage daughter is asleep on the sofa, schoolbooks on her lap. Mom is distraught, dejected, despairing—so much to do, so little time.

Me, I would have danced. The house is immaculate! My daughter is asleep! The schoolbooks are decoys, but who cares! I found perfect greens! And I've got real wood furniture! Even if it's only for a photograph!

What the image portrayed was a day in the life of bland, boring, predictable Christian suburbia, a metaphor for bland, boring, predictable faith. That wasn't the intention, but that was my take-away. This is the way good Christians are supposed to look, and this is what happens when we try to do too much; surely, the cover seemed to say, you can relate. If you can relate—if I can relate—then we're in a pretty sorry condition. Because relating to this image would mean that our faith has become suburban, languishing in a safe and sterile setting. And we have become domesticated and easily dismayed when our choices disrupt our routines and mar the perfect pictures we've painted.

Frontier faith—wild, intense, fierce faith—cannot grow in a suburban spirit. It lies dormant, buried deep within as a haunting, distant memory of a fiery spiritual desire that first attracted you to God. Like a geographic frontier, frontier faith lies just beyond the edge of a settled area, beyond suburbia, beyond the outlying rural regions. Its terrain is unpredictable. There's no telling what lies ahead, but that's the point. Not knowing and yet trusting is what defines faith.

Restoring the frontier faith that fueled your first love for God will bring you closer to fulfilling your haunting spiritual desire, even as it distances you from those who are determined to hold tightly to their suburban spirit. But it's OK. Your feeling of alienation may finally fulfill its intended purpose.

∞

> The desert and the parched land will be glad;
> the wilderness will rejoice and blossom.
> Like the crocus, it will burst into bloom;
> it will rejoice greatly and shout for joy.
> *Isaiah 35:1*

Lord, I'm asking You to demolish any remnants of a suburban spirit in me and restore the frontier faith that first drew me to You. Keep my faith wild, intense, and fierce, for the sake of Your kingdom.

A VOLATILE AND TOXIC BREW

Whenever two men meet there are really six people present.
There is each man as he sees himself, each man as the other
sees him, and each man as he really is.

WILLIAM JAMES

*S*exist language aside, the nineteenth-century philosopher William James nearly got it right, but he omitted one crucial duo—each woman as she thinks the other sees her. These eight "people" create quite a volatile and toxic brew; think witches and cauldrons and all kinds of nasty stuff bubbling to the surface. It's really a wonder we get along with anyone at all.

Shortly after I graduated from college, I ran into a college buddy that I hadn't seen for some time. We started out in the same graduating class, but unlike me, she managed to make it through in four years without having to take time off to get her head straight. As she approached me, I smiled but stiffened. Denise knew me way back when, and "when" had been a rough phase in my life. Seeing someone from that time, someone who knew the reckless, out-of-control me, caused me to retreat back inside myself. The only "me" Denise knew was the one I wanted to forget.

Explaining that I was on my lunch break from work, I quickly updated her on my life and let her do the same, but I wasn't about to start reminiscing. As I turned to walk away, she mentioned that she had gotten together with a mutual friend the week before. "Your name came up, in fact," she said. "We decided you were the most together person we knew the whole time we were in college." Good grief! I had been a borderline mental case! In making that observation about me, they had not only besmirched the good names of all the other people we had known in college—people who really were together—but also they had tarnished my onetime opinion that they both had good sense. Clearly, they were delusional.

No one has it all together. Much closer to the truth is that each one of us has got it together in some ways, and each one of us does not have it together in other ways. The sad fact is that when we get too close to acknowledging our own soundness—the solid and together parts of who we actually are—our discomfort with finally dredging up something good causes us to retreat. We cloud our thinking with layer upon layer of crummy and often false perceptions of what we think other people think about us. We create our own volatile and toxic brew.

We cannot see ourselves as we truly are; we can only come just so close, as if we are seeing a poor reflection in a mirror. But we can also stop assuming we know how others perceive us. That many "people"—those eight perceptions stemming from just two individuals—muddy the image even more. It may just be worth it to hold our perceptions until the day when we can know even as we are fully known.

> Now we see but a poor reflection as in a mirror; then we shall see face to face. Now I know in part; then I shall know fully, even as I am fully known.
>
> *1 Corinthians 13:12 (NLT)*

Lord, keep me from assuming what others think of me—but also keep me from caring too much about their opinions. Because Yours is the only one that counts.

YOUR LOT IN LIFE

Complaining about our lot in life might seem quite innocent in itself, but God takes it personally.

Erwin W. Lutzer

Honestly, you would think that we humans, with all our higher-level intellectual skills and sophisticated cognitive abilities, would be just a tad more appreciative of the way God put us together. Even with my limited understanding of the animal kingdom, I'm pretty certain that giraffes don't complain about their unsightly necks, elephants about their leathery skin, or hogs about their obvious weight problem. No, you don't hear animals uttering a single complaint about the way they're made, with the possible exception of cats, but they hardly have what you'd call a strong case.

In all my years of complaining about my appearance, which pretty much stopped after I had children and my priorities started to straighten out a bit, it never once occurred to me that I was leveling my complaints against the God who created me. A simple exercise in logic would have led me to that conclusion, had I applied it: I believe God made everything, which logically includes me; therefore, when I complain about who I am and how I look, I'm offending—who? The God who made me. I ought to know better than to file a complaint against Him, as we all should. Because God does indeed take our complaints personally, as He showed time and time again with those recalcitrant Israelites, His ever grumbling chosen people.

So I eventually stopped complaining about my appearance, but it took a much longer time for me to stop grumbling about my nature and all those alienating, quirky traits that I cannot change for all the world. I'd stand in church, and right along with the best of them I'd sing all these choruses about how God was the potter and I was the clay, and He would mold me into what He wanted me to be. Well, He'd already done that once, and given those results, I didn't exactly sing those songs with much enthusiasm or optimism. But I didn't think I was blaming God for the way I had turned out; after all, I had heard flesh-and-blood potters talk about lumps of clay they'd tried to work with that seemed to have minds of their own, and I figured I was a stubborn, independent lump. It took way too many decades for me to acknowledge that the Master Potter was not only trying to shape my will and my character on a daily basis, He also was expecting me to stop trying to fit my true nature into a mold that did not suit me.

The choice that confronted me was an obvious one: Continue to complain, and find out what it's like to have God for an enemy (Numbers 14:34), or stop complaining and avoid dying in the wilderness, possibly by being swallowed up by the earth (Numbers 16:32). Accepting the way He made me suddenly seemed doable, if not attractive.

You don't really want to discover how God will react when He begins to take your complaints personally. You might want to opt for the alternative: appreciating the way He made you and staying on His good side by never again asking, "Why have You made me like this?"

∞

But indeed, O man, who are you to reply against God? Will the thing formed say to him who formed it, "Why have you made me like this?"
Romans 9:20 (NKJV)

―――――――――

Lord, I thank You for the way You have made me—quirks and all. Keep me from complaining about my lot in life, the lot that You personally chose for me.

CONTAINING MULTITUDES

Do I contradict myself? Very well; I contradict myself.
(I am large, I contain multitudes).

WALT WHITMAN

It's really no wonder people think I'm crazy sometimes. I'll be engaged in some spirited conversation about, say, a recent movie, and I'll go on and on about how much I enjoyed it and why, and maybe a month later I'll be engaged in another spirited conversation with the same person, and I'll go on and on about how much I hated that same movie and why. "Do I contradict myself? Very well, I contradict myself," I wish I could say. But no. I don't remember brilliant lines like that at appropriate moments, like when someone points out one of my many inconsistencies. Instead, I gaze off into space, trying to pull out of the air the memory of our earlier conversation or the reasons for my earlier opinion.

It's no use, though. Because I am so prone to mental lapses, I often feel as if I'm force-feeding my mind, stuffing in far too many thoughts and impressions out of sheer terror that someday the lapses will take over. So I try to stay ahead. As a result, my long-suffering brain contains a multitude of inconsistent opinions, facts, and memories that I've inflicted on it, just as my soul contains the innumerable contradictory impressions and wordless intuitions that I've imposed on it. But capturing it all and keeping it all sorted out is too heavy a demand, and I end up appearing to be either muddleheaded or dishonest. I'm neither, at least not due to my contradictions; to quote another poet, "I'm not confused. I'm just well-mixed." I like to think of myself as being as well-mixed as Robert Frost was.

It's likely that you've contradicted yourself on more than one occasion, though maybe not in the same way I described. It's possible that someone has accused you of being a pathological liar or a basket case, all because you're filled with overlapping perceptions that don't necessarily line up when you give voice to them. But you are large, and you do contain multitudes, because you live deeply. How do I know? Offbeat people can't help but live deeply; it's in their nature. The depth of your thinking alone would drive a lesser person to the edge of a cliff—and beyond.

Living with your contradictory nature can be maddening, especially if your significant other or someone equally close delights in pointing out your incon-sistencies. Oh, just go ahead and let them have their picky little pleasure. You do contain contradictions, because you contain so much. Accept it and admit it to yourself, and when others point it out, cheerfully agree, throwing a bit of Walt Whitman or Robert Frost at them, if you like. And remember to return the favor when others contradict themselves.

I have thought deeply about all that goes on here in the world, where people have the power to hurt each other.

Ecclesiastes 8:9 (NLT)

Lord, don't allow me to let other people get to me. More important, remind me to cut people some slack when their inconsistencies begin to show.

A TIDY SOUL

Be careless in your dress if you must, but keep your soul tidy.

MARK TWAIN

*E*lijah the Tishbite already was a man of some reputation by the time he delivered a message of doom to King Ahaziah in the first chapter of 2 Kings. The unsteady Ahaziah had been injured in a fall, and he wanted to know if he would survive. But instead of asking the God we know and love, he sent his messengers to the dreaded Baal-Zebub, the god, albeit false, of Ekron. On the way, the entourage encountered a man who blasted Ahaziah for sending them to a false god and prophesied that Ahaziah would indeed soon see his end. "What kind of man was it?" the king asks, when the messengers returned. "A hairy man wearing a leather belt," he was told. You can almost see King Ahaziah stroking his beard as he solemnly intoned: "It is Elijah the Tishbite."

Now one less-than-scholarly commentary suggests that the reason Elijah was so easily identifiable by such a brief description is because all he was wearing was that leather belt, which I'm thinking must have been very, very wide. On the contrary, most scholars agree that the belt was indeed an accessory item; "hairy," they maintain, refers to his tunic and not his body, which means he wore actual clothing. A rough and hairy camel-skin tunic would have identified him as a prophet; the words he spoke, with their telltale lack of a positive spin, would have narrowed the list of potential prophets down to Elijah. Regardless, Elijah's physical appearance was somewhat like that of a madman; good grooming was apparently not high on his list of daily priorities. But the man could call down fire from heaven like nobody's business, and that's just what he did on this auspicious occasion. Oh, and as predicted, Ahaziah died soon afterward.

Like John the Baptist and a host of other men and women of God, Elijah marched to the beat of a different drummer in the biblical fashion parade. You get the impression that he was so caught up in his current mission from God that he completely disregarded all those pesky little details that other people seemed obsessed with, like wearing normal clothes. Now, I've never done the Elijah thing, and I happen to be exceedingly fond of clothing comfort, but sometimes I do get so wrapped up in what I'm doing that worrying about my appearance is way down on my list of priorities. I'm always clean, and I think I'm always neat; I'm just not well put together. No makeup, indistinct hairstyle, "scary" clothes, as a member of my public once noted.

If you march to a different fashion beat, you've gotten your share of unkind looks and comments. Ah, but is your soul tidy? Not tamed but tidy—washed and pressed and ready for the next mission God has for you? That's all that matters, of course. Your public may not forgive you your fashion indiscretions, but just wait and see how impressed they are when you call down fire from heaven.

∽

But the Lord said to Samuel, "Do not consider his appearance or his height, for I have rejected him. The Lord does not look at the things man looks at. Man looks at the outward appearance, but the Lord looks at the heart."

1 Samuel 16:7

Lord, show me how to keep my soul tidy, washed and pressed and prepared for whatever mission You have for me. And give me eyes to see other people as You see them, not as the world sees them.

THE WEAKEST PART

Certain defects are necessary for the existence of individuality.

JOHANN WOLFGANG VON GOETHE

What's your most troublesome defect, the part of you that psychologists might call the weakest part of your character? Is it some peculiarity that you believe keeps you from fitting in? Many of us would immediately name a problem connected with our discomfort in social settings. Everyone else in the room may think they're at a dinner party, but we know the truth: "Dinner party" is simply a euphemism for "chamber of horrors." Trying to engage in the requisite small talk is pure torture for the likes of us; unfortunately, torture is an efficient if cruel means of determining what a person is made of.

You're probably a pretty decent person when it comes right down to it, but a single social blunder can leave you decimated, convinced that you're a fool to think you could ever show your face in public again. You feel hopelessly trapped in what you perceive as the weakest part of your character. Your particular defect could be the transparent way you exaggerate to make your life sound more interesting or the overly assertive manner in which you express your strongly held opinions. Our weaknesses are as individual as we are, but their effect on us is pretty much universal. They make us miserable.

If you're feeling trapped by anything that denies who you are inside—any behavior that makes you feel crummy about yourself at the end of the day or the end of the dinner party—then there's a great deal of hope that you can find your emotional freedom. There's hope because you have identified the problem and admitted it, always a huge first step toward recovery—not recovery from your misfittedness but from those things that make you feel wretched because you're still on a misguided mission to try to fit in.

Defects serve a purpose in our lives, not only for the existence of individuality, as Goethe pointed out, but also as a reminder that God alone is perfect. It's an acknowledgment of God's perfection that prompts a devout needleworker to intentionally skip a stitch or a pious calligrapher to purposely mar a letter. Most of us have no need to make such deliberate errors, whether it's in our work or in our character; we produce flaws quite nicely on our own, if we do say so ourselves. We'll never be free of defects.

The apostle Paul flat out delighted in his weaknesses, because he knew that he could rely on God to be strong in those areas where he was weak. Relying on God to be our strength is no excuse for refusing to change what can be changed, but there's a great deal of comfort in knowing that God will be our strength as we try to change our changeable weaknesses and learn to accept our unchangeable defects.

෴

That is why, for Christ's sake, I delight in weaknesses, in insults, in hardships, in persecutions, in difficulties. For when I am weak, then I am strong.

2 Corinthians 2:10

Father, let this familiar prayer become fresh in my spirit once again: Grant me the serenity to accept the things I cannot change, the courage to change the things I can, and the wisdom to know the difference.

IN HOT WATER

To be right with God has often meant to be in trouble with men.

A. W. TOZER

If you were fairly alert during the early 1980s, you may remember one of Ayatollah Khomeini's short-lived darlings, Abolhassan Bani-Sadr, the first president of Iran and the first to be driven out of office by Khomeini. His utterly lyrical name—pronounced "ah-bull-hahssen-bonnie-sodder"—would roll off my tongue at the most inappropriate of times. Who cared? I loved saying his name. I still do.

Which brings me to Sanballat, a Persian official who served as the governor of Samaria five hundred years or so before the birth of Christ. There's no connection between him and Bani-Sadr that I'm aware of. I've just wanted to use Sanballat's name for a long time, and A. W. Tozer—no lightweight in the name department himself—provided this golden opportunity. Because Sanballat was one of the many ruling men that the Jewish people found themselves in trouble with over the biblical years. Think Herod and John the Baptist, whose head was served up on a platter because he dared to speak the truth. You get the idea. The Jews were frequently in hot water.

Sanballat specialized in imposing a different kind of trouble on the Israelites, the kind we're mostly likely to face on a regular basis: ridicule. His target was Nehemiah's crew of construction workers, a group of devout Jews who had been given permission to rebuild Jerusalem's walls, which were in disrepair following the exile of the Jewish people from the city a century earlier.

With the support of a couple of neighboring bullies, Sanballat greeted the crew with derision. (I imagine him as an arrogant Disney villain: big guy, huge stomach, deep laugh, haughty and mocking and scornful, scantily clad in that way Walt's animators have with Middle Easterners. But maybe that's just me.) His derision turned cruel once he realized that these Israelites were serious about the responsibility God had placed in their hands. "What are these feeble Jews doing? . . . Will they revive the stones from the heaps of rubbish—stones that are burned?" (Nehemiah 4:2 NKJV). Later, Sanballat resorted to force to try to stop the rebuilding of the wall.

What's especially important for us in all this is the Israelites' reaction to Sanballat's taunting. When the strength and resolve of the workers began to falter, Nehemiah reminded them of their "great and awesome" Lord and encouraged them to keep up the fight for what they knew God had directed them to do. They got back to work, persevered through one Sanballat-ordained obstacle after another, and completed the job.

Whenever God gives you an assignment that is big or foolish or impossible to accomplish, you will face all manner of ridicule, insults, and rejection. You're already accustomed to dealing with that on a smaller scale, but now that there's something larger at stake, your resolve needs to be stronger than ever. Can you withstand even more ridicule? Of course you can. In fact, you can even "rejoice and be glad," knowing that your great reward will eventually be handed over to you. And your here-and-now reward—being right with God—isn't all that shabby either.

∞

> "Blessed are you when people insult you, persecute you and falsely
> say all kinds of evil against you because of me. Rejoice and be glad,
> because great is your reward in heaven, for in the same way they
> persecuted the prophets who were before you."
> *Matthew 5:11–12*

Lord, thank You for giving me not only the strength to withstand ridicule but also the grace to rejoice when being right with You means being in trouble with other people.

ETERNITY IN EACH MOMENT

You must live in the present, launch yourself on every wave,
find your eternity in each moment.

HENRY DAVID THOREAU

Steve is one of those rare people who has learned—or perhaps he would say, is learning—to live in the present moment. So committed is he to the concept of intentional living that a while back he abandoned a typical American lifestyle in response to a call from God to a radical lifestyle of hospitality and spiritual direction. As a director of a tiny community of believers in a rural area, Steve is responsible for everything from cooking and cleaning to serving the Eucharist. He lives alone in a small cabin on the property.

Watching Steve prepare a meal for retreatants is like watching Steve prepare the Eucharist; he approaches both responsibilities with a sacramental reverence. It seems to not matter at all how often Steve has prepared and served the same meal, just as it clearly does not matter how often he has served the bread and wine. Each meal he prepares, whether at the stove or the altar, carries with it a freshness and a newness, as if this is the first time he has cooked dinner or served the Eucharist, and not, perhaps, the hundredth.

It's people who live on the edges of society who seem most attracted to a purposeful, intentional way of living. Although it's a challenge, many of those people continue to live in the cities and the suburbs and go about their daily work as toll collectors and CEOs and bureaucrats and ski instructors. But the way they live and the way they work reflects a fundamental shift that separates them from our anxiety-driven, high-speed, gotta-get-it-while-you-can culture. Their every task is offered up as an act of devotion to God and service to humanity.

Intentional living forces us to slow down, and it's right there that many of us get stuck. I know how hard it is; mine is a deadline-driven profession, and the word *sacrament* hardly applies when I find myself in a frenzied bind with two or three major projects coming due at once. On the contrary, the words that apply in those situations are the kind I wouldn't use in polite society, words that I didn't even realize I knew anymore. But my—our—inability to live sacramentally is hardly proof that it's not a viable way to live.

James 4:14 is not what I would consider to be a particularly inspiring Bible verse. If we recognize the truth in it—that we are but a mist that appears for a little while and then vanishes—and refuse to be discouraged by it, then that truth can prompt us to live in the present. No, we don't know what will happen tomorrow. That's all the more reason why we should approach both our mundane and significant tasks in a sacramental way, giving ourselves over to the task of folding the laundry with the same reverence we give to folding our hands in prayer.

෧෨

Why, you do not even know what will happen tomorrow. What is your life? You are a mist that appears for a little while and then vanishes.

James 4:14

Lord, teach me to live intentionally in the moment, to give myself over to the routines and tasks of each day as if they actually counted for something. Help me eliminate those things that count for nothing.

WILD FAITH

He did not say, "You shall not be tempted;
you shall not be travailed;
you shall not be afflicted." But He said,
"You shall not be overcome."

JULIAN OF NORWICH

Medieval women of faith must have kept the prevailing religious authorities on their toes; tales of mystical wild women abound in the accounts of eccentrics and ascetics and the like who lived during the Middle Ages. Julian, whose real name no one has ever discovered, was one of these wild women—wild in the sense that she embraced an expression of faith that could not be confined to the conventional.

Ironically, she herself was confined, voluntarily, in quarters that were equally unconventional: a tiny sealed cell attached to a wall of a church in Norwich, England. The room most likely had three windows, one that looked into the interior of the church, one for the delivery of meals, and one for visitors who sought spiritual counsel from her. Her only companion was a cat, and its only function was to keep the rat population down.

But within the confines of that small room, Julian would experience a series of mystical encounters with Christ that influenced countless believers over the five centuries since her death. Her book, *Revelations of Divine Love*, considered by many to be the first great surviving book written by a woman, stemmed from her unusual prayer request that she be allowed to share in the fellowship of Christ's sufferings through bodily illness. During the nearly fatal illness that followed, she experienced a vision of Christ's crucifixion that had such a profound effect on her that it formed the basis of her meditations and writings for the next twenty years.

Julian knew what it meant to be tempted, travailed, and especially afflicted. But she also knew what it took to be an overcomer. Through prayer and contemplation—and the insights she gleaned from her vision—Julian experienced the intensity of the love of God and recognized that intense love as the power that overcomes the world.

We may not be able to comprehend what it is that drives a person to a life of such extreme rigor, but we can appreciate the wisdom Julian mined from the richness of her time alone with God. We can know the intense and powerful love of God without sealing ourselves in a tiny cell with a cat, and we can draw on that love when the rats out there start to get to us. If you're feeling defeated, give all that you are over to the passionate love that God has for you; seek your own revelation of His divine love. He has promised that He will not allow you to be overcome by the world.

⊚⊚

For everyone born of God overcomes the world. This is the victory that has overcome the world, even our faith. Who is it that overcomes the world? Only he who believes that Jesus is the Son of God.

1 John 5:4–5

Father, I thank You that the power of Your divine and eternal love enables me to overcome all the temptations and sufferings that life may bring. Keep me mindful of that love.

BELIEVING THE BEST

I always prefer to believe the best of everybody—
it saves so much trouble.

RUDYARD KIPLING

I once worked for a guy whose self-esteem was so diminished that the only way he could feel good about himself was to think the worst about other people, which usually meant his employees. You'd go about your work knowing there was a cloud of suspicion over your head, but you could never figure out what you were suspected of. Far worse, though, was finding out. That happened to a friend of mine, several years after she left the company on what she thought were good terms. But no. She ran into this guy—a.k.a. the man of the perpetual sneer—and he came right out and told her that he always thought she had cozied up to certain clients in an underhanded and unethical way. He chose to believe the worst about her, even though no one had uttered a single word against her. His suspicions were all formed and locked up in his inscrutable mind.

Like my friend, I can take a lot from other people. I'm pretty thick-skinned these days. But like her, when I discover that someone has thought the worst about me—without ever providing me with details or hard evidence or even a chance to defend myself—my nose gets decidedly out of joint. Laugh at me, ridicule me, mock me, but don't ever, ever call my integrity or my professionalism into question. You *will* hear from me.

Of course, that places squarely on my back the exceedingly annoying burden of believing the best about my accuser. Don't you wish certain demands in life didn't work both ways? If I want someone to believe the best about me, then I have to believe the best about him. All right, all right, I concede. But I admit I'd be tempted first to immerse myself in a brief but satisfyingly vengeful fantasy, followed by a period of heartfelt repentance.

Believing the best about others doesn't just save a lot of trouble. It also releases us from the burden of exacting judgment and vengeance on others. God is clear in warning us about what we can expect if we persist in judging others, and it's not pretty. We're going to get exactly the same form of judgment that we've so readily dished out on other people. "Vengeance is Mine," He reminds us in Deuteronomy 32:35 (NAS), freeing us from the consequences of judging and condemning others.

If you haven't grown a fairly thick layer of skin already, you're probably overdue. God wants you to understand that as long as you let other people get to you, they will get to you. You have the ability to stop the cycle of believing the worst about those who believe the worst about you. Ask Him for the grace to live as Jesus did, relentlessly loving the very people who thought the very worst about Him.

෨෨

"Do not judge, or you too will be judged. For in the same way you judge others, you will be judged, and with the measure you use, it will be measured to you."

Matthew 7:1–2

_____

Father, give me the grace to always think the best about other people, bearing in mind that the judgment I inflict on them will only come back to haunt me. Thank You for releasing me from the burden of having to exact vengeance on others.

WE'RE STILL CHILDREN

We do not cease to be children because we are disobedient children.

FREDERICK DENISON MAURICE

The year had been a particularly bad one for the parents in our church—the parents, that is, of children who were now adults. Many of the middle-aged and elderly mothers, in particular, shouldered burdens that kept them pretty close to the brink of despair. Not only were they having to deal with their children's broken marriages and alcoholism and occult practices, but also many of them faced the everyday reality of a new threat on the horizon—AIDS. Far too many of their children were engaging in unsafe, promiscuous sex. The fear of the parents, who were trying so hard to trust God through all of this, was palpable.

One Sunday morning, our pastor interrupted his sermon on hope right after commenting on the fear he sensed among the parents in the congregation. "Those of you who have adult children that you're praying for, children who have left the faith or never embraced the faith and are now living apart from God, I want you to stand," he said. The rest of us sat and watched as these grieving parents stood, some hunched over with the weight they were carrying, some doing everything in their power to keep from crying. The pastor's next words, in which he encouraged those standing to never give up hope, seemed to offer little consolation. But then he continued: "Now, those of you who were once wayward children, who in your adult years had strayed far from God but have since returned, I want you to stand." As dozens of us rose to our feet—yes, of course, I was part of the second group—he said, "Moms, Dads—there's your hope."

Well! I'm not one to break down and cry in church all that often, but as each wayward child found a grieving parent nearby, we collapsed into each other's arms and pretty much cried for the rest of the morning. And I can't think of too many church services that I'd call unforgettable, but that service was an exception. It was a remarkable experience.

Sometimes when we've strayed from the Father, we keep right on straying because we've managed to convince ourselves that He is so displeased with us that we're as good as disinherited. If the Father is that mad at us, there's no hope of reconciliation, is there? So we sink deeper and deeper into sin. Of course, we didn't bother to consult with God about His alleged displeasure and decision to disinherit us. He still considers us very much His children. He's just waiting for us to return to Him, so He can enfold His loving arms around us once again.

The adult children of those grieving parents never for a moment stopped being sons and daughters. No matter how far they had wandered from their faith or their family, no matter how ungodly their lifestyles had become, they remained children whose parents loved them. To paraphrase the words of Jesus in Matthew 7: If these parents, being flawed humans, could so love their disobedient children, how much more does Your merciful Father in heaven love you?

Just as you who were at one time disobedient to God have now received mercy as a result of their disobedience, so they too have now become disobedient in order that they too may now receive mercy as a result of God's mercy to you.

Romans 11:30–31

Father, Your love—and Your willingness to forgive—is incomprehensible. After all I've done to You, You still love me. Remind me of Your love when I'm once again tempted to stray from You.

THE BEAUTY OF HOLINESS

He that sees the beauty of holiness, or true moral good,
sees the greatest and most important thing in the world....
Unless this is seen, nothing is seen that is worth seeing: for
there is no other true excellence or beauty.

JONATHAN EDWARDS

*L*ike lots of kids who grew up on the wrong side of the tracks, I developed quite the fantasy life. For several years, I had an imaginary friend, presumably to replace my friend Sharon, who had moved to another town. My mother humored me by setting a place for her at meals, though I'll bet it was my father who got to eat her dinner. In time, I put away childish things. No more imaginary friends for me. I had graduated to the next level, in which I laid claim to imaginary ancestors, the most auspicious of which was eighteenth-century minister Jonathan Edwards.

That wasn't as far-fetched as it seemed. Edwards is my maiden name, and I was a maiden at the time. Plus, he was from New England, and I had actually visited New England. I so wanted to believe that I was descended from this brilliant man; I didn't know all that much about him, but it was enough to know that he had entered Yale when he was thirteen and that he could preach up a storm. I could go for years on those two facts alone; they were a whole lot more respectable than any facts I had about my real, nonimaginary, lower-middle-class family.

Edwards had a lot to say about holiness, proof positive that my claim was a lie. (Then too, his descendants included college presidents and professors, lawyers, judges, doctors, prominent authors, senators, and a vice president—not a single glassblower in the lot. And I come from a long line of glassblowers. There you go.) But holiness doesn't get a lot of press today, and when it does, it isn't good press. Holiness gets linked to austere nineteenth-century women in long black dresses preaching against the evils of alcohol or the dangers of gambling. Few people today would think of holiness within the context of beauty.

I suspect that those of us who feel like outsiders would be in for a shock if we were to truly devote our lives to developing holiness as a character trait and a lifestyle. We would find out quickly enough what it really feels like to be treated as an outcast. And yet God considered holiness to be not only important but also attainable, by giving all that we have and all that we are to God, staying current with our confession of sin and the resulting repentance, and maintaining our relationship with Christ as both our Savior and our Lord. It's not all that complicated, but then again, it's not all that easy. We just need to see the beauty in it to appreciate its worth—to God and to our lives on earth.

Give unto the Lord the glory due to His name;
Worship the Lord in the beauty of holiness.

Psalm 29:2 (NKJV)

Lord, bring me around to a more accurate understanding of holiness. Let me experience firsthand what it means to worship You in the beauty of holiness.

THE RHYTHMS OF YOUR SPIRIT

*As I made my way back to church, I began to find that many
of the things modern people assume are irrelevant—the liturgical
years, the liturgy of the hours, the Incarnation as an everyday
reality—are in fact essential to my identity and survival.*

KATHLEEN NORRIS

discovered spiritual memoirist Kathleen Norris around the same time I discovered the fictional twelfth-century monk Brother Cadfael, the main
character in a book series by Ellis Peters and a PBS series based on the books.
Norris's description of contemporary monasticism captivated me. Her stories—
like the one about the monk in South Dakota who pulled a loaded gun from
under his mattress and leveled it at a suddenly repentant burglar—breathed
life into a group of people who for too long have remained mysterious and misunderstood. The PBS adaptation of Peters's books did much the same, human-
izing those men and women who are too often perceived as otherworldly and a
bit unreal.

Never one to allow myself the pleasure of pure entertainment, I became so
intrigued by medieval monasticism in particular that my bookcases began to

emit a peculiar groan under the weight of my newly acquired tomes on medieval spirituality, and my house began to resemble a Cadfaelian cloister. So I went a bit overboard, but what I thought was an interest in ecclesiastical history led me to discover a place in the contemporary church where my spirit finally found a home. To my astonishment, I found that the structure provided by the liturgy of the Anglican Church became, as Norris described it, essential to my identity and survival.

Perhaps it was moving to Florida from the Northeast that made me ultimately crave the rhythms of the liturgical year, rhythms that I never even knew existed until recently. Ever since our family relocated from Delaware, I've been thrown off balance by Florida's version of seasons. In our part of the state, we have two seasons: mowing and no mowing. Our "no mowing" season lasts a few months, and then it's back to cutting our acre of grass every other day or so. I yearn for the rhythms of a year in which there's a first frost and a spring thaw; a warm, sand-colored summer and a crisp, brilliantly hued fall. I suppose it was only natural that once I realized that there were people alive today who actually lived by the rhythms of the liturgical year, I would find my place among them.

Paying attention to the rhythms of your worship style can help you find your place in the family of God, even if that place is far removed from the liturgical setting in which I discovered my place. Your worship life may move to a salsa rhythm or a techno rhythm, a country rhythm or a classical rhythm; we already know that it moves to an alternative rhythm. Like me, you may not even know where your spirit will find its home until you have opened yourself up to something completely new, which in my case meant a liturgical expression that I had wrongly been led to believe was lifeless and sacrilegious and, most heinous of all, liberal. That's where I fit, and it took the better part of my life to find that out.

Relentlessly pursue your place in God's family. Allow Him to lead you to that place, even if the path you have to take is unfamiliar and perhaps a bit scary. Finding your spiritual home may prove to be essential to your very identity and survival.

಄

My spirit finds its joy in God, my Savior.
Luke 1:47 (GOD'S WORD)

Father, let me never be satisfied until I find my place in Your family on earth. Keep me open to following You, even if You lead me to unfamiliar places.

THE REWARD FOR CONFORMITY

The reward for conformity was that everyone
liked you except yourself.

Rita Mae Brown

*E*ileen is one of those people that you either love or you hate, which means she's something of a prophet. Not the kind of prophet who can accurately predict the future, though she's done that on more than one occasion, much to the chagrin of her prophetic victims. Rather, Eileen is the kind of prophet who accurately sizes up a situation in your life by determining the hidden forces at work. And then, of all the nerve, she slams you with the truth about your life that you thought you had so carefully hidden. This would account for the love-hate thing; few people can stand on middle ground when she lets loose.

Well, I'm among those who love Eileen, partly because she has saved me from myself several times and partly because she's shorter than I am, which is about the only advantage you can have over her, but you take what you can get. After she got me to quit smoking and drinking myself to death, I figured we were cool. What was left? Plenty, and she unearthed it all, like this sickening need that I had to be liked by everyone.

Like many of her prophetic utterances, this one came as she was cutting my hair; I think she purposely saved up her heavy-hitting words for moments like that, when her victims were most vulnerable. We were chatting away, or so I thought, when I mentioned an incident at church with someone whose facial expression betrayed her obvious dislike for me. "What on earth did I do to her?" I asked—rhetorically, I thought. But no, Eileen shifted her weight, a sure sign that she had slipped into Jeremiah mode. "Hurts to realize you're disliked, doesn't it?" she said, with more than a hint of sarcasm in her voice. If I hadn't been sitting down, and vulnerable to the mercy of scissors in the hands of an angry prophet at that, I would have imposed my full five-foot-three-height on her right there and then. But I sat, and she blasted. Who did I think I was? What made me think everyone should like me? Did I consider myself that special? Clearly, for some time, Eileen had been thinking about me and my pathetic need to be liked.

Conforming to the subtle psychological demands of any group will almost inevitably lead you to a place of self-loathing. You compromise so much of yourself and make so many accommodations to fit into the group that you end up a fraction of the person you once were. And you wonder how things got to be like this, how you arrived at a place where you feel disconnected and uncomfortable in your own skin.

Some people will simply never like you, for reasons you can't fathom and maybe they themselves don't even understand. Others will like you and love you and possibly adore you, and that's the group you will find yourself in once you stop jumping through ever higher and higher hoops to try to be likable. Finally, there's the vast majority of people you'll meet in your life, those who shrug you off and don't think one way or the other about you. Unless, of course, you're like Eileen.

We are made right in God's sight when we trust in Jesus Christ to take away our sins. And we all can be saved in this same way, no matter who we are or what we have done.

Romans 3:22 (NLT)

Lord, keep me from being so concerned about whether people like me that I try to be someone I am not, someone You never made me to be.

THE VALUE OF GOD'S LOVE

———————

God does not love us because we are valuable.
We are valuable because God loves us.

MARTIN LUTHER

In the town where my daughter lives, there's this winsome little band of professing saints who stand on a downtown street corner every Friday afternoon and pass out tracts, or at least attempt to. They're usually somewhat less than successful, which could have something to do with the placards they carry that bear such inspirational slogans as "Turn or Burn!" and "Fly or Fry!" Right on the corner where they stand is a store that carries all sorts of occult paraphernalia. As I unflinchingly pass by my alleged brethren, I'm often tempted to walk right into that den of commercial iniquity. I'm not saying that I've ever given in to this temptation and bought a candle just for the fun of it or anything. Or that once inside the store I've discovered all kinds of anti-Christian bumper stickers that I'll bet the store wouldn't have stocked had it not been for the street performers outside.

When you witness this kind of battle, you know that each camp feels decidedly superior to the other—the Christians because of their vengeful God, the

Wiccans because of their powerful goddess. Meanwhile, real live people are in need of a real live Savior that the Wiccans in the store don't recognize and that the Christians on the street corner have managed to obscure, despite their obvious advantage in the truth department. What both camps are missing is the reality that their value as human beings has nothing at all to do with whether they are right or wrong. Their value has everything to do with God's love for them.

The street-corner Christians lost their edge the moment they began focusing on their beliefs rather than their Lord. Part of what they believe—but only part—is that sinners will burn in hell. I'm fairly certain they also believe in the love of God, but they've forgotten how extensive that love is, that His love crosses every barrier. And that includes the threshold to each and every magic shop.

The Wiccan who owns that downtown store has just as much value in the eyes of God as you or I or the street evangelists do, because she is just as much His creation as we are. That may cause a few self-righteous backs to stiffen, but it should have just the opposite effect. We can relax in knowing that it's God's love that makes us worthwhile, not anything we do or say—or fail to do or say. His love is eternal and unchanging, which means that our value to Him is also eternal and unchanging. That's a bit much to take in, but to believe in the veracity of the Bible is to believe in the unfathomable love of God.

When we keep our focus where it belongs—on who we believe in rather than on what we believe—we learn to recognize the value of every individual, and our witness to the world becomes grounded in love. Because God, of course, is love itself.

෨෧

We love Him because He first loved us.
1 John 4:19 (NAS)

———————————

Father, remind me of the value of every human being, no matter how different or misguided they may be. And keep reminding me that I am of value if for no other reason than for the simple fact of Your love for me.

ALTERNATIVE WORK STYLES

*Few people are capable of expressing with equanimity opinions
which differ from that of their social environment.*

ALBERT EINSTEIN

f you've ever expressed an unpopular or a minority opinion—and I have no doubt that you've expressed your share—you're aware of the kind of repercussions your words can have. In a social setting, you're looked upon as an oddity at best. But in a work setting, the consequences can be severe. Educational institutions in particular can be unforgiving of the brave soul who dares to challenge the status quo, but corporations and businesses in the private sector can be just as merciless. You can compromise, of course, making everyone but yourself happy. But you do have another option: You can change your environment.

Though my reasons for leaving a traditional job were varied and complicated, one fact was clear: I was not cut out for corporate life. Neither my life rhythms nor my right-brained tendencies could be confined to a typical 9-to-5 format. Trying to fit in was making me and everyone around me miserable. When other factors combined to make traditional work difficult, I took advantage of the opportunity to get out. And I've never looked back, even as we attempted to adjust to an unpredictable income and even when some of my clients—Christian publishers—stiffed me. Freedom always comes at a price, and I have learned that I am willing to pay it.

It helps that I'm highly self-motivated and that my line of work is conducive to self-employment. But alternatives to traditional employment exist in just about every field. Educator Parker J. Palmer discovered this when he was offered a faculty position at Georgetown University shortly after he had reached the conclusion that he was born to teach but not in a traditional setting. This would have presented quite a dilemma had it not been for Georgetown's flexibility: It turned out that the university wanted Palmer to work with his students out in the community rather than in the classroom—as part of an experiment in, as Palmer describes it, "education unplugged." It was an experiment that proved to be satisfying and successful.

Your inability to fit in at work can be just the catalyst you need to explore alternative work opportunities. You'll probably have to make some sacrifices, not the least of which is the measure of security that a steady paycheck brings. But does it really? With all the downsizing and mergers and fluctuations in management style, no one's job is ever all that secure. More important, Jesus is supposed to be our security. Leaving the traditional work force will expose just how much you have learned to depend on Him; for a time, you may realize how much more you had come to depend on your employer. Granted, it's much easier for a single, childless person to strike out on her own, but plenty of parents, including single mothers, have found a way to preserve their identity, sanity, and income through alternatives to 9-to-5 jobs. Give yourself permission to explore alternatives to a job where you just don't fit in. Some people will think you're crazy, of course, but that's probably nothing new. What appears to them to be a foolish move could in fact be one of the wisest steps you've ever taken.

But God chose the foolish things of the world to shame the wise;
God chose the weak things of the world to shame the strong.
1 Corinthians 1:27

Lord, keep me from settling for second best if my only reason for doing so is the fact that I've placed my trust in job security rather than in You. Lead me to what You know is best for me, no matter how frightening it may look at first.

ONLY THE LONELY

*How touching it must be to a soul, coming in fear
before the Lord, to feel at that moment that someone is
praying for him, too, that there is still a fellow
creature on earth who loves him.*

FYODOR DOSTOYEVSKY

I used to find a great deal of comfort in the first part of Psalm 42, verse 7, which reads: "Deep calls to deep." That verse would conjure up the awesome and comforting image of the Spirit of God communicating with my spirit on a level that I was barely aware of. What's more, the verse held out hope that my spirit was able to communicate on a wordless and deeply intimate level with another human being, a real live kindred spirit.

On a human level, I've discovered that there's good news and bad news in that. The good news is that the spirit of one misfit is like a powerful magnet that attracts other misfits, which means we can count on meeting people of like mind. The bad news is that the spirit of one misfit is like a powerful magnet that attracts other misfits, which means we can count on meeting people who are downright scary.

Like stalkers. I've known several of those, but one in particular really gave me the creeps, even though she was probably the least harmful of the lot. This painfully lonely young woman would appear out of nowhere, startling the day-lights out of me as I walked to work or sat at a table in a luncheonette near the office. She seemed to know when I would be leaving for the day, even though my hours were unpredictable, and she'd fall in step with me out in the street. Her crooked half-smile and haunting, imploring eyes did nothing to endear her to me, nor did her tendency to seriously invade my personal space. I would be only as nice to her as I felt I had to be—minimally courteous, just cordial enough to show God that I was trying. And I'm sure I prayed for her, because this was at a time when I actually kept a prayer list. I would pray a quick prayer for each name on the list and check it off to prove I had done my duty and, I suppose, to make sure I didn't waste time praying for the same person twice in the same day.

Eventually, my stalker stopped appearing, and I forgot all about her. I wish now that I hadn't, but I was so relieved to be rid of her that it was easy to dismiss her from my mind. How could I have known then that I would one day experience such a measure of loneliness that I would become clinically depressed and even suicidal? Her intense loneliness was just plain creepy to me at the time.

I hope that today I would treat a misfit like her with a greater measure of compassion. Instead of adding her name to a ridiculously long prayer list, I hope I would go before the Father on her behalf with such a depth of love and understanding that she would know that someone somewhere was pleading her case before the throne of God. And I hope that would make all the difference in the world in her life.

We may feel that there's not a whole lot we can do to make life easier for people who are so socially crippled that they even manage to alienate the alienated. But we can pray for them—really, truly pray for them. Not just add their names to a prayer list, not just check off their names once we've met our minimal obligation in prayer, but go before God on their behalf in compassionate and loving intercession. I may be wrong, but I have a feeling that God might give us an idea or two about other ways we could make a difference in their lives. An unsettling thought, to be sure, but intercessory prayer tends to produce those.

And pray in the Spirit on all occasions with all kinds of prayers and requests. With this in mind, be alert and always keep on praying for all the saints.

Ephesians 6:18

Lord, never again allow me to turn my back on a lonely person. Give me a greater measure of love and compassion for those who bear their own brand of misfittedness.

THE GREATEST MYSTERY
WRITER OF ALL

When I was young, I was sure of everything; in a few years,
having been mistaken a thousand times, I was not half so sure
of most things as I was before; at present, I am hardly sure
of anything but what God has revealed to me.

JOHN WESLEY

ecently, I read a short story by mystery writer K. T. Anders called "A Sim-ple Matter of Training." All too often, the works that some authors con-sider mysteries aren't; halfway through, you know whodunit, and your momentary surge of pride at having figured it all out is tempered by the distinct feeling that you've been cheated. *If you're such a hotshot mystery writer,* you think, *how come I knew the ending at the midway point? You're supposed to be better at this than I am.* But Anders pulled a "Gotcha!" on me, and the delight-ful twist at the end of her story so took me by surprise that I realized how rarely that has happened. I actually smiled as I read the final line.

As good as Anders is, she's no match for the greatest mystery writer of all time and beyond, God Himself. The author of such titles as *The Great Mystery of Life* and *The Great Mystery of Faith* has this uncanny ability to pull a divine "Gotcha!" on us just at the point where we think we've got it all figured out. And no one is better at surprise endings than He is.

Though it's a flawed analogy, going through life is in many ways like reading a promising mystery. As young children, many of us were blessed with a fine-tuned sense of wonder. Life seemed to hold a limitless supply of opportunities for exploration and discovery and fantasy—until the day arrived when we were pretty much told to put away childish things. Life became scientific and mechanistic and, worst of all, filled with certainty. We learned that the earth *would* spin on its axis every twenty-four hours. And with that fact, the sun "rising" in the east—what faulty science those primitives embraced!—would cease to hold its wonder for us.

We spent countless years stuck in the mire of unquestioning, resolute conviction about the way it's supposed to be. But then, little by little, we sensed that we were beginning to lose our equilibrium, which had never before failed us. Many of the certainties of our lives became fuzzy, and we began to experience "Hold it!" moments: *Hold it! That's not the way life is supposed to be!* or *Hold it! That can't be what Jesus meant!* or *Hold it! Professional athletes can't go on strike!* From the profound to the mundane, one sure thing after another morphed into a red herring.

Eventually, if we're smart, we fall in step with John Wesley. We look back on a thousand times when we were mistaken, shake our uncertain heads in disbelief, and admit that the only things we're sure of anymore are those things that God has revealed to us.

To truly love life, you've got to love the mysteries it contains. It's pointless to try to figure it out, because God's got more "Gotcha!" moments in store for you than you can possibly imagine. Me, I'm looking forward to the surprise ending, the one that theologians are so sure about but can't seem to agree on. I have this feeling that the twist at the end will bring a smile to a multitude of faces.

> Forget the former things;
> do not dwell on the past.
> See, I am doing a new thing!
> Now it springs up; do you not perceive it?
> I am making a way in the desert
> and streams in the wasteland.
> *Isaiah 43:18–19*

Lord, thank You for keeping the mystery in life. You've given us so many surprises to look forward to. Restore to us the sense of wonder we lost so long ago.

SPIRITUAL WANDERINGS

Not all those who wander are lost.

J.R.R. TOLKIEN

One of the curses-disguised-as-blessings in my life is my inability to get really and truly lost. I admit it comes in handy sometimes, and when you come right down to it, I guess I have to count my navigational skills among my blessings. But honestly, just once, when the stresses of life get to be too much and I want to disappear for a while, I would love to take off for a few days and claim that I got lost. But alas, that is never to be, because no one would believe me. Other than the week I spent trying to find my way out of Boston one day, I cannot recall ever being lost, which of course says as much about Boston as it does about me.

But I love to wander. When I was in college, I would get in my car and meander throughout the Northeast, sometimes with a destination in mind, sometimes without any idea where I was going, but seldom would I take a direct route. Now that my children are older, I'll occasionally go away by myself—my husband being a die-hard stay-at-home type—and explore new areas, turning on to any road that piques my curiosity. One of my longtime dreams is to drive across the country and back without ever using an interstate highway, though I'm not sure that's a physical possibility anymore.

It's when I start to wander spiritually, though, that my well-meaning sisters and brothers in Christ start to worry that maybe I'm genuinely lost this time. I'm about as orthodox as a Christian can be, but when I dare to cross a denominational line or other artificial spiritual barrier, well, that can only mean one thing: I've clearly lost my way. To those who obsess over the condition of my soul as they stand on the sidelines and watch in horror, I can only say one thing (politely, of course): Get over it.

If we know the truth, then the truth can set us free to explore new ideas, new worship styles, new methods of biblical interpretation, new ways of expressing our faith. Without abandoning that truth, the truth of the gospel, we can indeed embark on a meandering, curiosity-driven faith journey without ever fearing that we will get lost. We have a navigator who is far more reliable than even the most sophisticated satellite navigation system on the market today; if we begin to stray off course, we can be sure we will hear a gentle and ancient voice behind us saying, "This is the way; walk in it" (Isaiah 30:21). What better guide could you ask for?

Wander to your heart's content. With the Holy Spirit as your guide, your faith journey is certain to be an adventure. Who knows where He may lead you? And all the while, you will be as far from lost as you can get, because you will be in the presence of the One whose purpose it is to safely lead you home.

∞

I know that you are with me and will keep me wherever I go, and will bring me back to this land.

Genesis 28:15a (NRSV)

Father, I know I can rely on You to never let me get lost. Thank You for making this faith journey that I'm on such an adventure.

FALLING IN HOLY LOVE

*Real prayer comes not from gritting our teeth
but from falling in love.*

RICHARD FOSTER

If you've been around evangelical Christianity for any significant amount of time, you've no doubt heard of the ACTS method of prayer. ACTS is an acronym for what many agree are the four essential elements of prayer, in their order of importance, no less: adoration, confession, thanksgiving, and supplication.

Over the years, I've probably tried every method of prayer out there, including ACTS, but I found I was concentrating more on the method than on the prayer. My breakthrough in prayer came when I realized that adoration pretty much covered all the other elements. Before any hackles get raised, of course, I agree that we need to give voice to our confession, our gratitude, and our requests. But the simple act of adoration—loving and praising God simply because He is God—covers a multitude of lesser concerns.

Our prayers of adoration bring us back to the point where we first fell in love with God, restoring to us the wonder and magnificence of that first taste of a pure and holy love. Our misfittedness melts; our defenses disappear; and our excuses evaporate as we spend time simply allowing our hidden soul, our conscious thoughts, and our spoken words to magnify the Lord.

For many of us, falling in love with God is something we need to do over and over again. In one sense—and perhaps only one—it's like falling in love on a human level. You fall in love, but after a while that falling sensation, the one that made your heart skip all those beats, levels off. You're still in love, and you're sure you will always love this significant other. But the thrill isn't the same—until one day, without any warning, you fall in love with the same person all over again, skipped heartbeats and all.

Each time we come before God in an attitude of prayerful adoration, we open up our hearts to the possibility of falling in love with Him all over again. And you know what happens when you fall in love. All those things that once seemed so important—in a godly context, that means all our petitions and supplications, our laundry list of needs that we intended to present to the Almighty—fade to insignificance. One thing, and one thing only, occupies our thoughts, our minds, our hearts, our very being, and that's the presence of our Beloved. For an all-too-brief span of time, we dwell in the reality that we need nothing else in life but these cherished moments with the One we adore simply because He is who He says He is. In those times, the peace that passes understanding would render us incapable of gritting our teeth, even if we wanted to. Which, of course, we wouldn't.

I love you, O LORD, my strength.
Psalm 18:1

Lord, I adore You simply for who You are and not just for all that You've done for me. I want to keep falling in love with You over and over again, never straying from that first taste of a pure and holy love.

JESUS WITH A BACKBONE

▬▬ ▭ ▬▬

*Our commitment to Jesus can stand on nothing less
than a recognition that he is the one who knows
the truth about our lives and our universe.*

DALLAS WILLARD

t's midmorning on a June day in 1958, and a dozen or so third graders find it impossible to settle down after their brief recess out in the church's playground. The teacher summons the children to take their places among a half-circle of chairs facing an easel. I sit in the front row, breathlessly hoping and praying that the teacher's next move will be toward the beloved flannelgraph and not the box of boring posters. Yesss! It's a flannelgraph day, and all's well at vacation Bible school.

Flannelgraph stories ruled my religious life in the late 1950s. The vivid colors of the figures, the texture of the cloth, the smell of the flannelgraph, and the changing scenery of the backgrounds all merged into one intoxicating sensory experience. I became heady with spiritual wonder the moment the teacher rested the flannelgraph on the rickety easel.

Ah, but flannelgraph figures had their dark side, just like so many seemingly innocent enchantments of my childhood. As innocuous as they appeared to be, the flannelgraph people became embedded into the psyches of all those spongy third graders, including mine. On into adulthood, we carried with us one image in particular, one that had the potential to do the greatest damage to our spiritual lives as adults—the image of Jesus. Flannelgraph Jesus was sweet and gentle and kind, and He had no backbone to speak of. Like all the other figures cut from felt, He'd flop right over the second you removed Him from the board.

Flannelgraph Jesus is far removed from the complexity and reality of who the Savior is. Yes, He's sweet, gentle, and kind, but He's got a backbone like no other. And He's fierce, powerful, and dangerous. "Safe? Who said anything about safe?" asks Mr. Beaver in C. S. Lewis's tale *The Lion, the Witch and the Wardrobe.* "'Course he isn't safe. But he's good. He's the King, I tell you." And as we learn later, He's strong and intelligent and all those other descriptors that accurately apply to Aslan, the Lion of Judah, Jesus.

Until we come to terms with the omniscience and omnipotence of the Son of God, we stifle His activity in our lives. We treat Him as a benign character in some long ago and faraway story, a somewhat weak, effeminate, and harmless moral teacher. Flannelgraph Jesus, through and through.

Scrap that image. Get embedded on your psyche the image of Jesus as strong, powerful, and mighty in every way—including intellectually. In *The*

Divine Conspiracy, Dallas Willard presents Jesus as the most intelligent man who ever lived. That image alone reduces flannel Jesus to shreds.

Next time you read the gospel accounts, read them with this image of Jesus in mind: Jesus as an intellectual giant, one who knows all there is to know about the operation of the universe and the inner life of every person who ever lived. Then make sure that your commitment to Jesus is resting firmly on that foundation, the image of the Son of God with one powerful backbone.

> For by him all things were created: things in heaven and on earth, visible and invisible, whether thrones or powers or rulers or authorities; all things were created by him and for him. He is before all things, and in him all things hold together.
>
> *Colossians 1:16–17*

Lord, thank You for freeing me from the false image of You that I carried from my childhood. Let me never forget that you are all-knowing and all-powerful.

RISKING IT ALL

Human beings all over the earth have this curious idea
that they ought to behave in a certain way,
and can't really get rid of it.

C. S. LEWIS

Dirk Willems was a Mennonite who lived in Holland in the sixteenth century, a lethal mix of belief, time, and location. To be a Mennonite at that time and in that place meant the threat of execution. When Willems's religious affiliation was discovered one winter, he was hunted down and pursued. He might have gotten away had he not been within earshot of the cries of his pursuer, who had fallen through a thin layer of ice. As a Christian, Willems knew he had to rescue the man; as a law enforcer, the official—grateful though he was—knew he still had to turn Willems in to the authorities. Several days later, Willems was burned at the stake for his faith.

Martyrs are the kind of people who have neatly disposed of the curious idea that they should behave in a certain way. Disregarding the value of their own life, they refuse to conform to the pattern of the world and instead submit themselves to the transforming power of God. A transformed Dirk Willems certainly got his opportunity to "test and approve the will of God" (Romans 12:2), and it cost him his life. To be transformed does not mean that you will be exempt from the consequences of your abnormal human behavior.

We could make a fairly strong case for the assumption that not all of us are called to behave in the radical way martyrs do; in fact, a strong biblical case could be made for Willems's not saving his pursuer. The Israelites were never directed to pull Pharaoh's drowning forces from the Red Sea; that thin layer of ice could easily be seen as a providential sign that Willems had nothing to fear. Or it could be that our thinking has become so conformed to the ways of the world that we immediately dismiss any possibility that would interfere with our safety or even our comfort.

I tend to think that our misfit nature is something of a setup for radical discipleship. God may have made us the way we are for "such a time as this" (Esther 4:14), a time when He would be looking for followers whose popularity, reputation, and standing in society are meaningless, if not worthless. We've already faced abandonment and rejection simply because of who we are; to face the same for the sake of the kingdom of God would almost come as a welcome relief. At least, we figure, our misfittedness would finally serve a purpose.

We all need to be disabused of the notion that we ought to behave in a certain way. Until we are transformed by the renewing of our minds, though, we will constantly be faced with the temptation to fit in, to conform to the ways of the world. But falling prey to that temptation is the way neither of the radical disciple of Christ nor of the martyr for the kingdom of God. The radical, transformed way is the way of the outsider, the outcast, the alien—the misfits that God has embraced and called to be His own. It's a calling that virtually defines our place in the family of God.

> Do not conform any longer to the pattern of this world, but be transformed by the renewing of your mind. Then you will be able to test and approve what God's will is—his good, pleasing, and perfect will.
>
> *Romans 12:2*

Lord, I want to be counted among Your radical disciples, those who risked it all for the sake of the kingdom of God.

The Author

$\mathcal{M}$ arcia Ford is a former religion editor for the *Asbury Park Press* in New Jersey, associate editor of *Charisma* magazine, and editor of *Christian Retailing*. In 1999 she launched her own successful writing and editing business, Ford Editorial Services, and since 2001 has also been affiliated with WordSpring Media. The author of *Memoir of a Misfit* and *Charisma Reports: The Brownsville Revival* and coauthor of *Restless Pilgrim: The Spiritual Journey of Bob Dylan*, she has written five additional published books.

Marcia and her husband, John, live in Central Florida with their daughter Sarah. Their adult daughter, Elizabeth, lives nearby.

Marcia would love to hear from other misfits. You may contact her at Misfit@marciaford.com.

Other Books of Interest

Memoir of a Misfit:
Finding My Place in the Family of God
Marcia Ford
$18.95 Hardcover
ISBN: 0–7879–6399–2

How many of us have, in Marcia Ford's words, "sacrificed pieces of (ourselves)" to find acceptance in the church? How many of us have suppressed our true stories, gifts, and even intelligence for the sake of fitting in? Marcia Ford's *Memoir of a Misfit* is the candid, delightfully irreverent journey of a woman determined not to settle for recycled faith.
—**Sally Morgenthaler**, author, *Worship Evangelism* and founder,
Sacramentis.com

Marcia Ford's funny, fresh, and frank memoir chronicles the spiritual journey of a self-proclaimed misfit. Like Anne Lamott, she is witty, quirky, and candid about her shortcomings and her sneaking suspicion that she may really be a square peg in a round hole. Equally reminiscent of Lamott's writing, it is through Ford's own uniqueness (her so-called misfittedness) that she is able to discover and claim God's abundant grace, and come to experience God more fully.

Like the author, many of us, especially women, feel as if we don't quite "belong"—not in society, due to seismic cultural shifts, and not even in the church. *Memoir of a Misfit* will help fellow misfits everywhere appreciate (and even relish) God's purpose in making us the way He did. Specific Scriptures, when viewed from the perspective of a misfit, coupled with personal experience and the wisdom of others, underscore the value of misfits and the special place we all have in the family of God.

MARCIA FORD is a writer, principal in WordSpring Media, and contributor to *Publishers Weekly* Religion BookLine. She has been an editor for *Charisma, Christian Retailing, Ministries Today,* and iBelieve.com. She resides near Orlando, Florida, with her husband and children.

[Price subject to change]